Ho[...]

Than[k you ...] encouragement [in] tennis and running. [...] great to see you coaching.

Randy Cook
April, 2014

IBSN-13 978-1497316409
IBSN-10 1497316405

Hip! Hip! Hooray!

I'm Running Again!

By Randy Cook

This book is dedicated to my wife and best friend, Debbie Dunn Cook. You encouraged me to write this book and made me the happiest I have ever been. Thanks for always being there for the good times and the surgeries. God sent me an angel.

To Greg Eck, the best running partner anyone could ever hope to have. Sadly, you are no longer here to revisit those incredible training runs. I miss you.

Foreword

He was a marathon man, that's for sure. I had heard of him, but we had never met; not face to face that is. We were acquaintances, found standing on the line knowing the other by shape alone with eyes down, shaking out arms and legs in anticipation. Together we surged forward. Sometimes he saw my back and sometimes I saw his. There was a bond created out of respect, for he knew I was like him. That was then.

I remember the day we came together for the first time; neither extended a hand, as we were competitors first and always. Our eyes met and we acknowledge each other with a nod. "How ya doing?" I blurted. He replied "good" and then we ran.

It was out of mutual need to escape loneliness that we tolerated each other. We were competitors. We set out to test, pushing hard, then harder, careful to avoid all out confrontation until we were both satisfied.

Then came trust - then, we spoke - questions first, then stories, then laughter. It was after the laughter that we became running partners.

From then on, we had each other's back. I looked forward to our meetings: 10 miles, 15 miles, and 20 miles; sometimes speed. We never stopped, limited water to one fountain, and never waited. If one's shoe came loose, it meant a 5:10 surge mile to catch up. I loved those meetings and soon learned to love the man.

Randy became my friend, yet we remained constant competitors, as if out of instinct. I liked it, but it ended like it started, suddenly. First came the fear of what might become, signaled by the taste of bile when legs are stolen. Knowing a hard charging, relentless Randy, it was not hard to grasp what became the runner's kiss of death. Like him, I didn't believe it at first. It would be a month, then three months at the most, then a year, and then we lost touch. We were friends through running and that was gone. 30 years have passed and now he is back. I write celebrating the return of my friend, and look forward to read the last chapter. It should be a great story.

Bill Bernard

As a member of a recently organized local running club (Tidewater Striders) in the early 1970s, I experienced my first competitive road race at age 35, and immediately fell in love with the sport. I had played football and wrestled in both high school and college and found that my competitive sport spirit was still alive. I wanted to run faster. About this time I met Randy Cook, who was in his mid 20s at the time and one of the fastest members of our running club in all distances from the 5K through the marathon. Several members of our club would get together occasionally for a training session on the cinder track at Old Dominion University, and I can recall trying to hang on to Randy as long as possible, usually only about 300 meters or so, as he did 800-meter repeats. Those training sessions helped Randy maintain his status as one of the fastest local runners, but also helped me become a faster runner.

Randy continued to compete, winning many local races both overall and as he aged, in the submaster category. He was also very successful as an age-group runner in state, regional, and national competition eventually meriting his election into the Tidewater Striders Hall of Fame. Then, all of a sudden, in the late 1980s he disappeared from the running scene.

As runners, we all know that all it takes is one small injury to derail our training and thus, our competitive running ability. Minor ailments such as a pulled muscle, an inflamed joint, or a bone stress fracture can put our training on hold, with subsequent loss of cardiovascular and metabolic efficiency so critical to efficient running. Fortunately, such injuries are normally short-lived, and we may resume training within a relatively short time frame and return to our normal running performance.

But, what if the ailment does not heal? What if the ailment is a bad hip joint? Or worse yet, both hip joints? As we all know, the hip joint is one of the most important for runners. It is the link between the leg and the torso. It bears the weight of our total upper body on impact during running. A chronically injured hip, much less two injured hips, would normally be the end of one's running career. Such was the case with Randy Cook, and he had to stop running due to the pain. Eventually both hips were replaced, the first in 1996 and the second about ten years later.

Randy had remained relatively active during the intervening years by coaching tennis at the high school level and serving as a high-level tennis referee. However, he missed one of the major passions of his life – running – and upon retirement decided to give it another try. He started slowly, and gradually improved his speed so he could race again, albeit as an older runner. This book describes the process of his remarkable recovery and his subsequent running experience.

Mel Williams

Table of Contents

Prologue

This book will take the reader from my 20 plus years of running at a very competitive level, suffering through numerous injuries and illnesses along the way, enduring two total hip replacement surgeries and missing 25 years of running and attempting a comeback in 2012.

What I will stress throughout this book is that regardless of what sport you are involved in, and this book happens to be about running, you will occasionally be faced with adversity. Every athlete will be injured at some time in their career; some minor and some more severe than others. The key thing to remember is that if you love running as much as I do, then you will persevere when you have small aches and pains, appreciate every day that you can run, and if you have a serious injury, "Don't give up, don't ever give up," as said by Coach Jim Valvano when he learned that he had cancer.

Chapter 1
Finding My Niche
1960 - 1964

"I run because I used to be envious of people that could run, and now I am that person."

Kendra Thompson

I was a late bloomer to the world of track and field and distance running. In high school I tried out for several sports to see if I could either make the team or if I could be good at a sport. Since I was only 5'9" and weighed 115 pounds as a freshman, I did not make the varsity basketball, wrestling, or football teams. I quickly learned that if I was going to succeed in sports it would have to be in an individual sport.

I made the swimming team as a breaststroker in my junior and senior years and earned a varsity letter. Since school started at 8:30, we practiced at the local Boys Club pool from 6:00-7:30 am, in January and February. The pool was heated, but the air was cold until the heater warmed up. By the time the heater finally did crank up practice was over. We ran from the pool to the locker room, took a quick shower then got to school just in time for first period. Our swim meets were in a small pool inside the administration building at Old Dominion College. I enjoyed the team concept and camaraderie, but swimming up and down the length of a pool and only seeing the black line on the bottom was not much fun for me. I needed to be outside so

I kept looking for a sport and not exactly making straight A's in the classroom.

This skinny, untalented kid spent four years in high school trying to find a way to fit in. If I had known about it or what it was I might have been a good candidate for the cross country team. I am sure we had a cross country team, but no one ever talked about it and it wasn't a glamour sport, so I never gave it a first thought let alone a second one. I did have some success as a tennis player while playing in local tournaments and Mid- Atlantic junior events. My parents wanted me to concentrate on tennis, but since we could not afford lessons it was difficult to compete with the guys who played year round and took lessons at Norfolk Yacht and Country Club.

I was taught to play tennis by my neighbor, Emmett Baise, at the Lafayette Park public courts in Norfolk. Emmett taught me the basics of the game and how to have fun. Mr. Baise was in his late 30s and I was 14 and it used to make me mad when he would use spin, slice, and drop shots that I could not get to. I vowed to get in better shape to be able to run down those shots.

Sometimes when I played in tournaments I encountered rude and arrogant kids. I see it much worse today now that I am a tennis official, however. When I was 15 I played in a tournament on the clay courts at the old Cavalier Country Club in Virginia Beach. My opponent hit a ball that went out, but he either did not like my call or was upset with himself, so he threw his racquet at me from one end of the court to the other. Thankfully it missed me by inches. In those days there were no USTA officials at the matches. All calls were made on the "honor system" and for the most part the players were honest. However, I was starting to think that tennis was not my sport.

Tennis is a very expensive sport and we did not have the extra money that was required for the cost of racquets, travel, lessons, entry fees, hotels, shoes, and clothing. In the spring of my junior and senior years I was a member of the Maury High School tennis team coached by Bill Brittingham, but I did not get to play in actual matches since I was not in the top six players in the lineup. At least I got to practice with the team and made some good friends.

Competitive running was the furthest thing from my mind in 1960. There were hardly any road races in the area and no running clubs. However, something happened in the fall of 1960 that got me interested in running.

I sat glued to our black and white television set watching Abebe Bikila of Ethiopia win the Olympic Marathon on the cobblestone streets of Rome while running barefoot. CBS Sports televised the race and it was the first time I had heard of the marathon let alone seen one on television. I was 12 years old at the time and I didn't see how it was possible for anyone to run 26.2 miles especially barefoot and close to five minutes per mile. The broadcasters did a good job of commentating on the race as it followed the lead pack through the streets of Rome. The marathoners started in Olympic Stadium for one lap of the track then ran through the streets of Rome, passing many of the ancient monuments and historic sites. I thought it was awesome to be able to see the ancient ruins at the same time the runners were competing. The audience was treated to views of Trevi Fountain, the Appian Way, the Roman Coliseum, and the Vatican. Bikila won the Olympics again in 1964 in Tokyo, but wore shoes in that race.

Was it just a coincidence that I would eventually become a World Geography and U.S. History teacher teaching about the ancient Romans? Later, when I served in the U.S. Air Force, I asked for and received Italy as my overseas duty station. I made sure to pack my running shoes. I found a store in Rome that sold Adidas running shoes, but they were made of leather in those days. They were guaranteed to give you blisters. I learned that the owners of the Adidas and Pumas shoe companies were brothers in Germany and had a falling out and went their separate ways and each started a company. I made several trips to Rome, Naples, Florence, Venice, and Pisa, in the eighteen months that I was stationed in Italy and used running as the best and fastest way to explore the cities.

I began to run around the block in the summer before my senior year in 1964 in my Chuck Taylor Converse All Stars to get in better shape for swimming and discovered that I enjoyed it plus I had some endurance. I would run once around the block fast, take a break, and then do it again and again. I didn't know it at the time, but what I was doing was what is called "interval training." I ran the 880 yard run in the Junior Olympics on the campus of Old Dominion College on a cinder track that summer and, even though I did not win a medal, I realized that if one worked hard enough they could be good at distance running.

I saw that running was something that a person could do anywhere and anytime and only required the basics of a decent pair of shoes, shorts and a shirt, and jacket in the winter. One didn't need a swimming pool or to find a tennis partner before you could get some exercise. Just go out the front door, run in any direction and you can get a fantastic workout and in less time. There are no membership fees or country club dues to be a runner either.

Chapter 2
The Old Dominion Years

1965 – 1966

"Good things come slow,
especially in distance running."

Bill Dellinger

When I graduated from Maury High School in June 1965 I was 5'10" and weighed 135 pounds. I wasn't very muscular but I had grown a little while in high school and had some endurance. I used to swim laps in the pool underwater and see how far I could go while holding my breath. I could easily swim 50 yards holding my breath.

From the 8th grade until I graduated I had a paper route to earn my own money. One good thing about the Virginian Pilot or the afternoon paper The Ledger-Star is that they made each carrier put $1.00 or $2.00 dollars a week into the "paper bank" and it could not be withdrawn until you quit being a paperboy. When I quit I had over $600.00 in the bank. So, I bought a used VW bug, paid for a semester of tuition at Old Dominion College, and bought some nice clothes for school. I was in high heaven!

I had absolutely no idea what I wanted to major in when I got to college. I knew that I liked sports even though I wasn't great at any particular sport. I wasn't a great student either because I worked on my paper routes either before or after school and it didn't occur to me at the time to study anymore than necessary to graduate with average grades. I loved my industrial arts and architectural drafting teacher, Mr. Christensen, and had visions of being an architect but I was poor in math. I considered being an industrial arts teacher like my favorite teacher, Mr. Christensen, but when I learned that I would have to take metal shop and wood working, I knew it wasn't for me.

So, in my freshman year at Old Dominion I took the basic math, English, and science courses and several activity courses in the health and physical departments. I started leaning towards being a health and physical education teacher and possibly a coach.

One afternoon I met Doug Mallory running on campus and we struck up a conversation. Doug ran track and cross country at Norview High School in Norfolk, VA. He talked me into running with him that fall, and as we got stronger and in better shape, we increased our mileage and added a variety of courses to our weekend training runs. We could be seen running in the Norfolk Botanical Gardens, Little Creek Amphibious Base, and from Old Dominion to Ocean View and back covering 10-12 miles.

In the spring of my freshman year in 1966, I made the Old Dominion College track team. Since this was the first time being on a track team, neither the coach nor I had any idea what my best event was. The coaches at Old Dominion at that time were Scrap Chandler and Lou Plummer, two living legends. They entered me in the 440 yard dash in some of the dual meets, but I found out that I did better in the longer events. A 59 second 440 yard dash won't win many college races.

In the summer of 1966, I was hired by Joe Thane to become a lifeguard and swimming coach at Mallory Country Club in Norfolk. I ran the six miles round trip to the pool everyday because I was going to try out for the cross country team at Old Dominion College. I would also run from Mallory Country Club to Norfolk Yacht and Country Club for swim meets then back to Mallory afterwards.

I loved running more and more and proudly wore the Old Dominion practice uniform that Coach Plummer gave me. I made the varsity cross country team and quickly learned what it was like to do running workouts at the college level. The hardest workout for me was 5 by 1-mile runs at race pace or faster with only a short rest period. Another hard workout was ten 440-yard dashes on the cinder track with short rest periods. These runs were always preceded by two miles of light jogging to warm up and another two miles afterwards to cool down.

My first race representing Old Dominion in cross country was a four-mile run on October 8, 1966, at Roanoke College in Virginia. I was scared to death because I did not have the experience of the other runners who had all competed in high school and I did not want to embarrass my team or myself. After training with the team for three weeks, I knew about where I fit in the pecking order of the other runners on our squad. I thought I could hang with Doug Mallory or Wayne Buyalos so that was my sole strategy, except not to drop out when I got tired. There was no way that I would ever let that happen. It was a fairly hilly course since Roanoke is near the mountains, so it was unlike anything I had ever run on. There is nothing except a small bridge to simulate a hill in Norfolk since it is at sea level. The miles quickly passed and I did the best I could to accelerate at the finish. I was exhausted after the race but once I caught my breath and took a hot shower I knew I had found my sport. I was able to stay with Wayne Buyalos the entire race and was only two seconds behind him at the finish. I was the 7th man on the team that day and my time was 22:13 or about 5:30 per mile average. Old Dominion defeated Roanoke College 15-50 (the low score wins in cross country).

On October 12 Old Dominion lost to East Carolina College 23-33. I was the 5th man on the team that day and my time for 4.5 miles was 24:45. My pace for this race was also 5:30 per mile and since it was a half mile longer I was getting better and stronger. I was also moving up in the lineup so I was feeling better about myself as a runner.

Old Dominion College defeated Washington & Lee 20-37 on October 15. I was the 5th man on the team again but my time for a very hilly 5.0 miles in Lexington, VA was 31:25 which is over 6:00 per mile. There was a hill that we almost had to crawl up twice but I did not stop and did not give up. I wasn't going to let myself or my teammates down. One thing for sure, I could not wait to get back to the flat streets of Norfolk.

Next, on October 18, we traveled to the University of Richmond and their beautiful but hilly course on campus with scenic loops around the college lake. We defeated the Spiders 19-37. I was the 6th man in this race and ran 22:32 for 4.1 miles which was 5:29 per mile pace. Teammate Wayne Buyalos beat me at the finish line by one second.

On October 21 Old Dominion hosted Bridgewater College and defeated the Eagles 20-35. Once again I was the number 6 runner for the Monarchs and ran 23:19 for 4.1 miles. In looking back I suppose the coaches were trying to toughen us up to prepare us for the conference and state championships coming up because we ran so many races so close together. The very next day we hosted Virginia Tech and lost to the Gobblers 26-30. Our number one runner, Pete Egan, ran faster than the day before but everyone else ran slower. On October 25 we ran against Randolph – Macon College on their 3.5 mile course and defeated them 19-41. I was the number six runner and my time for 3.75 miles was 20:31.

The Old Dominion College cross country team closed out its dual meet season on October 28 with a 15-44 victory over visiting Lynchburg College. My time for the 4.1 mile course was 23:45. On November 5, 1966, Old Dominion won the Little 8 Small College League Cross Country Championship at Bridgewater College. We next competed in the Virginia State Cross Country Championships in Blacksburg on November 11, and finished in 4th place behind William and Mary, Virginia Military Institute and Virginia Tech. The Monarchs finally closed out our season on November 19 at Washington College in Chestertown, MD, for the Mason – Dixon Conference Championships.

We finished in 2nd place behind Catholic University.

My lone cross country season at Old Dominion College was considered a success by Coach Plummer. Plummer said "We had six wins and only two losses, to East Carolina and Virginia Tech. Led by co-captains Wayne Buyalos and Pete Egan and team members Randy Cook, Andy Kowalsky, Doug Mallory, Wayne Veryzer, Charles Brake, Dave Sarrate, Tom Smith, and Larry Vann, we placed first in the Little 8 Meet, fourth in the Virginia State meet, and second in the Mason-Dixon Conference." I earned a varsity letter sweater in my first collegiate season of cross country. I had found my sport, or running found me, but either way I was hooked.

In looking back at our schedule I cannot believe we ran so many races and so close together. Ideally it is best to only race once a week and Saturday would be best so we would have time to study. Racing more than two or three times a month is inviting an injury. I think we each had our own jar of Atomic Balm to rub on our legs.

I was now ready for my first road race. On December 3, 1966, I ran in the Virginia Amateur Athletic Union 20K (12.4 mile) Championships in Williamsburg, VA. The race was three loops through the campus and woods around Lake Matoaka. I finished in 12th place and got a 5" plastic trophy that I still proudly display. I also got a medal for being on the winning team. I was looking for more races to compete in.

Chapter 3
From Boston to Serving Uncle Sam

1967 - 1971

"When you run in places you visit, you encounter things you'd never see otherwise."

Tom Brokaw

On January 7, 1967, I drove my VW bug an hour and a half to Ahoskie, NC, for the 2nd Annual Ahoskie Runathon 5 Kilometer Run. When I arrived I was asked to run on the Vann Track Club team from Ahoskie. I placed 5th overall in the 5K in 16:56 and was the number one runner on my new team. However, we lost to Hargrave Military Academy.

It is important to know that in the 1960s and up to the mid 1970s road races were few and very far in between. There was no Tidewater Striders Running Club, or Peninsula Track Club that had races. A runner had to be willing to travel sometimes great distances to find competition and even then the number of runners in most races was small.

All of this changed after 1972, when American Frank Shorter won the Olympic Marathon in Munich, Germany and placed second in 1976 to relatively unknown East German, Waldemar Cierpinski in Montreal, Canada. Cierpinski, like dozens of former East German athletes, was later found to have used performance-enhancing drugs, but was not disqualified. Shorter led a movement to get the East Germans disqualified and stripped of their medals, but it became too controversial and nothing became of it. As Olympian Grete Waitz of Norway said, "I have bad feelings, it wouldn't be fair for everyone. Let history be history."

In 1966, Bill Bowerman, coach at the University of Oregon, along with cardiologist W.E. Harris, published a 90-page book titled *Jogging*. The book sold over a million copies and was credited with igniting the jogging phenomenon in the United States. The running boom was accelerated with the printing of the book *The Complete Book of Running* by James Fixx in 1977.

With the leadership of Jerry Bocrie and Mel Williams the Tidewater Striders was formed in 1972, and has become one of the largest running clubs in the United States. The "Striders" have expanded to include a youth running team called New Energy that have weekly workouts in four local cities that attract hundreds of kids and dozens of volunteer coaches. The Tidewater Striders also sponsor triathlons, races for walkers, and a new group called POWER where able bodied runners push handicapped children in races. Now there may be two or three races on a given weekend and every organization or school PTA want to get in on the action and have a "fun run" for a fund raiser.

The first marathon ever held in North Carolina was the Durham to Raleigh Marathon run on January 28, 1967. Three members of the Old Dominion College cross country team entered the 26.2 mile race. Pete Egan, Doug Mallory, and I started the run which traveled the old Raleigh highway and finished at Reynolds Coliseum on the N.C. State campus. The Raleigh News and Observer reported that "the course was hilly and extended through the Research Triangle, Morrisville, and Cary" and "only 10 of the 17 runners who started the race finished." I finished in three hours and 22 minutes in my first marathon for 7th place. Pete Egan was 9th place in three hours and 25 minutes, and Doug Mallory unfortunately did not finish. The winner of the race was Bruce LaBudde of Atlanta who had previously won the Atlanta Marathon. His winning time was two hours and 36 minutes. In second place was Ed Hereford of Seymour Johnson Air Force Base in 2:43, third was John Osborne of East Carolina College in 2:49, and Pete McManus of N.C. State University was the 4th runner under three hours in 2:52.40.

After completing this marathon, Wayne Buyalos, another member of the Old Dominion cross- country team, and I signed up for the Boston Marathon to be run on April 19, 1967. The Ledger-Star, the local afternoon newspaper, wrote an article about Wayne and I training for the Boston Marathon. The article published on March 21, 1967, was titled "Road Runners Solve Traffic Problem … They Just Run."

So, on April 18, I got on the Greyhound bus in Norfolk for the trip to Boston. Wayne Buyalos was supposed to get on the bus in Newport News but never showed up. There I was all alone in Boston and had no idea what to do or where to go. I was relying on Wayne since he had been there before. We had planned to split the hotel bill so now I was worried how I was going to pay the exorbitant cost of $33.00 for two nights at the Lenox Hotel in Prudential

Center. The race had a record number of entries in 1967 of 735 (195 more than the year before). Fortunately, many of the runners were staying at my hotel so I just made sure that I was in the lobby early the next morning so I could follow the crowd to get to the right place.

On the morning of the race we were bused to the starting line in Hopkinton. All runners had to go to the small high school gymnasium and take a quick physical before receiving our race number. The race was started by the firing of a musket and the crowded streets of the small town started to thin out.

This was my first time running the Boston Marathon so I knew nothing about the course. The first few miles were downhill so most of us thought this was going to be easy. When we reached Framingham and mile six, the course leveled out. When I reached the half-way mark just before Wellesley College with the screaming female college students, my time was 1:30 and I thought I could be under three hours.

Little did I know that the dreaded "Heartbreak Hill" was looming near the 20 mile mark. This is actually a series of hills that begin at about the 17 mile mark in Newton and end near Boston College. There is a saying in marathon running that "the last 6.2 miles are harder than the first 20 miles." As a fairly new runner I learned this the hard way. After reaching the crest of Heart Break Hill the course leveled out and even had some slight down hills. However, I was just trying to reach that finish line in Prudential Plaza. I finished in 258th place in three hours and 20 minutes.

There were 600 finishers which was a record at the time.

Katherine Switzer made headlines the next day when it was learned that a female ran the race. She became instantly famous when a photo of race official, Jock Semple trying to pull her off the course made the front page of newspapers around the world. Switzer ran the race surrounded by a barricade of Arnold Briggs, Everett Rice, and boyfriend Thomas Miller.

Semple was knocked down by Miller when he got out of the press bus and angrily tried to pull Switzer out of his race. The bodyguards protected Switzer all the way to the finish line in approximately four hours and 20 minutes. Supposedly she entered under the name K. V. Switzer and had someone else take the physical for her so that she could get a race number.

Katherine Switzer became a heroine for all female runners because she did not give up that day in Boston. She persevered and continued to train for future marathons. She ran twice a day and as many as 110 miles per week in winning the 1974 New York City Marathon. Switzer ultimately ran a personal best of 2:51 at Boston in 1975. She believed that race validated her status as a serious athlete.

In addition to Switzer, Roberta Gibb, a spunky redhead, trotted across the finish line to the approval of the sleet-soaked crowd. She placed unofficially in about 280th place in 3:27:17. Gibb admitted that she jumped in the race about 300 yards from the starting line so she was not officially entered and thus did not have a race number. When asked if she wanted to be an official entrant, Gibb replied: "It doesn't matter. It's just fun to race."

Race director Will Cloney later said, "I'm terribly disappointed that American girls force their way into something where they're neither eligible nor wanted. All rules throughout the world bar girls from running more than a mile and a half." Cloney added that Switzer did not need to be disqualified because "she was never entered." Adding that "she got the entry number falsely and never took the required physical examination."

At this time the longest race for women was the 880-yard run which is one half mile. It was believed that it was dangerous and physically harmful for females to run anything longer than that. I am sure that Mr. Semple did not want a female to pass out or die while he was in charge of the race. There was not an Olympic Marathon for women until 1984 in Los Angeles, won by American Joan Benoit Samuelson.

The winner of the 71st Annual Boston Marathon in 1967 was David McKenzie of New Zealand in 2:15:45. McKenzie broke the record of 2:16:33 set in 1965 by Morio Shigematsu from Japan. Second place was Tom Laris of New York in 2:26:48, third was Yutaka Aoki from Japan in 2:17:17, fourth was Lou Castagnola from Washington, DC in 2:17:48, and rounding out the top five was Antonio Ambu from Italy in 2:18:04. Castagnola was a former runner at Old Dominion College.

The lives of thousands of young American men changed drastically in the mid 1960s with the war in Vietnam and I was no different. In the beginning of the war in Vietnam, students were given a 2S student deferment, but as the war escalated they began drafting young men even if they were enrolled in college.

In the spring of 1967, I took the test for the U.S. Air Force. However, little did I know that I would be on a waiting list that would last for months and that I could be drafted in the meantime. In May, I received a call from the recruiter saying that he could swear me in now and I would leave in two weeks or I could leave in a few days. My mother was on the other phone line and said "get him out of here now!"

I took a bus to Richmond, VA, and was inducted into the U.S. Air Force on May 22, 1967, for a four year stint. Several of us were flown that night to San Antonio, TX, for six weeks of basic training and arrived about midnight. When I stepped off the plane the heat and humidity almost gagged me. We were taken to the chow hall for breakfast at 1:00 am, then shown to our barracks. We finally had lights out about 3:00 am. However, to harass us there were four fire drills in the next two hours just as we got back to sleep. Reveille was at 5:30 am so we were totally exhausted the first several days before we got caught up on our sleep and adjusted to life as a recruit.

I was incredibly lucky to get in the Air Force when I did because I received my draft notice the first week of basic training. This almost certainly would have meant going into the Army or the Marines then off to Vietnam.

Needless to say, my running and training took a back seat while I was in basic training. I am serious when I say that I got out of shape during basic training. The Air Force basic training program was a joke compared to the Army or Marines. In the first week of Physical Training we ran ¼ mile a day. By the end of six weeks we had to be able to run one mile faster than 8:00. Anyone who could not do this would fail basic training and would have to stay for a few more weeks of additional physical training and be sent to the "fat boy squadron" as it was known. These lucky boys did nothing but run, run, run and do sit ups and pushups. I had no extra time or energy to run on my own so my running shoes were packed away for the time being.

After completing basic training I was sent to technical school at Keesler Air Force Base in Biloxi, MS, to learn Morse code and typing. I met Jim Colpitts, an Air Force officer stationed at Keesler AFB who had just finished the Boston Marathon in 24th place in two hours and 31 minutes. I tried to run with him on a few occasions but he was way out of my league. Jim introduced me to road races in New Orleans and we ran several 5-mile races during the six months I was stationed there.

In January of 1968, I was sent to San Vito Air Station in Brindisi, Italy, for eighteen months. I was fortunate to meet Dudley Godoy, another runner stationed there from California. We often ran together in the countryside and vineyards outside this small town in the heel of the Italian boot. We didn't think anything about running in the soft ground of the nearby vineyards until one day we were met by armed guards on Vespa motor scooters who were guarding the vineyards with shotguns strapped to their backs. When they saw that we were just two skinny runners and not someone trying to steal their grapes they let us leave. However, I learned my lesson and decided never to run in the vineyards again. This was just like a scene out of the movie The Godfather when the Sicilians were guarding Michael Corleone.

It was difficult to find the time to run on a regular schedule since I worked various shifts for twelve days in a row then I had four days off. During those four days off I frequently took trips to Corfu, Greece, on the ferry from Brindisi in the spring and summer months, or took the train to the major cities of Italy. When I traveled I always made sure to pack my running shoes so I could see more of the sights in a shorter period of time.

Dudley Godoy and I placed first and second in a 1,500 meter run at a sport meet at the small town of Latiano, Italy, in December 1968. 1,500 meters is slightly less than one mile so it was almost a sprint race for me. The U.S. Air Force Stars and Stripes newspaper headline in December 1968, read "Americans Dominate Long Distance Run in Italian Competition."

The article went on to say that "Godoy edged teammate Randy Cook in the 1,500 meter run as the two athletes from the 6917th Security Group finished first and second in a recent sports meet in Latiano, Italy." We competed against The Liberatas Sports Club of San Vito dei Normanni, Italy, at a sports day gathering attended by athletes from many of the local communities.

As a surprise to us, we had to run with waxed torches since the race was run on the dark streets of the Italian community behind a police motorcycle. There were sixteen of us runners with torches in hand who took off at the whistle. I managed to stay at the front of the pack with several of the Italian runners. With a quarter mile to go it was down to one Italian runner, Dudley Godoy and me, as the other runners began to fade. In the homestretch, Godoy showed that he still had plenty of reserve stamina and put on a burst of speed to pass me just before the finish line.

Dudley and I were selected to represent the U. S. Air Force in the European Armed Forces Championships in Wiesbaden, Germany. We rode the train from southern Italy all the way through the Alps. It was an honor to represent my Air Force Base in this competition. Dudley ran the one-mile and I ran the three-mile race. Neither of us placed in the top three in our event to win a medal, however.

My next and last duty station was Goodfellow Air Force Base in San Angelo, TX. I arrived there in August of 1969, just in time for the 100 degree daily temperatures. Now that I had a regular work schedule I upped my mileage and tried to run on a regular basis. Since I had been in the military for a few years and had served overseas, I was a bit of a rebel. Some of us veterans no longer starched our fatigues, just washed them and shook them when they came out of the dryer.

The base was very small so I would often run out of one gate for a 10-12 mile run then come in the gate on the other side of the base. Once I came in the gate with my shirt in my hand because it was so hot and I ran right past the MP. He yelled at me "Hey you, get back here!" I was thinking he wanted me to just put my shirt back on so I did then started running again. Now he was really ticked off and said "Halt or I will shoot."

Well, I stopped on a dime and went back to him. He asked for my ID which, of course, I did not carry with me. Then he asked what unit I was in. The MP then called my captain and said "I have a wise guy here named Sergeant Cook with no shirt, no ID, and he needs a haircut. Come and get him." My captain came and vouched for me and actually thought it was pretty funny. I did get a haircut the next day and started carrying my ID when I ran off base.

The highlight of San Angelo, TX, was the annual Rattlesnake Roundup in the spring. The locals would go to the caves and places where they knew the snakes to be and brought them in burlap bags to the auditorium downtown. Then they put them in a large circular ring made to hold the snakes. Handlers with high rubber boots would wade among the snakes and pick up one snake at a time and milk it for the venom. Then it was killed and the local Jaycees would sell you a meal of rattlesnake steak and two sides for $5.00. I understand that rattlesnake meat is quite tasty, but not for this city boy. I was too queasy just thinking about it to want to venture downtown and see this event in person. I saw it on the local news and that was more than enough for me.

My third marathon was the Kansas Relays Marathon on April 18, 1970, in Lawrence, KS. I ran two hours and 50 minutes and got 6th place. There were twenty finishers in the race. The winner was Chuck Ceronsky from St. John's College in Minnesota who ran 2:29:04. Second place was Brendon O'Shea from Nebraska in 2:32:01, third was Jeff Wray from the University of Kansas in 2:38:46, fourth was Carl Owczarzak from Kansas in 2:39:16, and rounding out the top five was Augustine Makil from Haskell Indian Institute in 2:49:44.

Then on November 21, 1970, I ran two hours and 49 minutes in the American National Marathon in Galveston, TX. Leonard Hilton from Texas won the race in 2:37:54. The entire race was run on the semi hard sand of Galveston beach in a straight line. Besides being extremely boring, my shoes slipped in the sand with every step and I had terrible blisters by the end of the race.

The war in Vietnam was winding down and President Nixon said that if someone in the military was accepted to a college they could be released up to four months early from the military. So, I jumped at the chance and was accepted to Angelo State College in San Angelo, TX, and was discharged on January 8, 1971. Angelo State had a track team but I had to sit out a semester since I was considered a transfer from Old Dominion College, even though I had not been there in four years. I trained with the team and did long runs on my own.

I met Joshua Owusu, a new member of the track team from Ghana, that spring semester. Since I was older than the other members of the track team I was asked to mentor him. Josh did the long jump, triple jump, and high jump, but was so good that he never had to practice when he lived in Ghana. Being on an organized team in the United States was very different for him. We kept in touch when I moved to Kansas for a few years and I even saw him at the National Track and Field Championships in 1973, in Arkansas. He competed in the long jump and triple jump and I ran the marathon. Joshua placed 4th in the long jump in the '72 Olympics and missed getting 3rd place and a medal by ¼ of an inch.

On March 6, 1971, I ran the White Rock Marathon in Dallas, TX, which was my fifth marathon. My time was two hours and 55 minutes and I was 7th place. The race was won by Rick Richardson of Arkansas in 2:38:09. We ran multiple loops around the lake in the premier of this race. This race has evolved to the point where thousands run the race and some of the top runners in the world come for prize money.

In the summer of 1971, I moved to Lawrence, KS, to be with my girlfriend who was a student at the University of Kansas. I got a part time job at Don Chilitos Mexican Restaurant and took some classes at KU. I met David Branson, a PHD student at the University of Kansas and a graduate of Pittsburg State University in Pittsburg, KS. David thought he could help me get at least a partial scholarship if I wanted to go back to school and run track and cross country. I had never heard of Pittsburg, KS, and had to find it on a map. I called the coach and arranged a meeting one afternoon in November. I made the two hour drive to Pittsburg and ran 12 miles with the team. I hung with the leaders and impressed Coach David Suenram. He offered me partial tuition, textbooks, running shoes, and help finding an apartment. With the $250.00 a month I received from the GI Bill, and a part time job on campus cleaning the football stadium, I was rolling in the dough. Oh, and Coach Suenram told me that it never snowed in southeast Kansas. What a joke that was! In the seven years that I spent as a student and teacher in Kansas, there was always a blizzard by Thanksgiving. I made the arrangements to move to Pittsburg and enroll there in the spring semester of 1972.

In September of 1971, I ran my sixth marathon at the Tri States Marathon in Falls City, NE. I ran two hours and 48 minutes and got 4th place. This scenic course started in White Cloud, KS, then crossed the river into Missouri then finished in Nebraska. The race was won by former University of Nebraska standout Greg Carlberg in 2:26:25, which broke the course record by four minutes. In second place was Lee Courcamp from Colorado in 2:38:41, third was Tim Hendricks of Peru, Nebraska in 2:38:57.

Chapter 4
The Pittsburg State Years

1972 – 1974

"Nothing's better than the wind at your back, the sun in front of you, and your friends beside you."

Aaron Douglas Trimble

I enrolled at Kansas State College of Pittsburg in the spring semester of 1972. This a lovely school with about 7,000 students in the southeast corner of Kansas, not too far from Joplin, MO.

In February 1972 I ran in the First Annual Heart Section Marathon in Pittsburg, KS. We started the race in Olympic fashion by running a lap around the college track then exiting the stadium and headed out to the gravel roads south and east of town. In this part of the country the roads are laid out in checkerboard style in mile squares called section lines. So, we knew how far we had run at the junction of every mile square. When we reached the half way mark we turned around and headed back towards Pittsburg. It was a typical winter day in February, that is cold and a strong wind out of the north. I finally made it back to the stadium where we ran one lap around the track then crossed the finish line. According to Gorilla track coach Dave Suenram, "Out of the 17 entrants, 12 finished the course. It was a hard day to run. In the last 12 miles the runners were going against a strong, cold north wind." I was not surprised that almost one-third of the field dropped out because it was so cold and windy.

The winner was Hank Brame of John Brown University in 2:38:09. In second place also from John Brown was Roger Lowe in 2:42:03. The third runner was Harry Lane from Haskell Institute, an Indian college in Lawrence, KS, in 2:46:22. I ran 2:56:39 and got 4th place barely beating Tom Anderson from Haskell Institute.

The Heart Section Marathon was never held again but whenever Coach Suenram sent us out for long runs it was always on the "marathon course." I have many fond memories of running on the flat gravel roads outside Pittsburg, KS. There were dozens of so called "strip pits" around town left from strip mining. They were stocked with fish and some people actually went swimming in them in spite of the danger of jagged rocks and holes.

My first cross country meet representing Kansas State College was in the Wichita State University Invitational in Wichita, KS, on September 16, 1972. Our team finished in second place behind a nationally ranked Wichita team. I was the 6th runner on the team but was very satisfied with my result.

On October 7, 1972, we defeated a strong Emporia, KS, State College team 22-33. Coach Suenram devised a strategy to defeat our rivals by holding our top runner, Mike Nixon back to pace the rest of the team for the first three miles then run the last two miles for the win. Nixon out sprinted teammate Tyler Todd by one second in running the five miles in 25:01. I was the 5th man on the team that day and 8th place overall and ran 25:47.

On October 13 Pittsburg State defeated Southwestern College of Winfield, KS, 15-48 with Nixon again winning the race. Mike's time for four miles was 20:06 and my time as the 5th man was 20:44. I was also 5th place overall in the race.

1972 was the year of "streaking" on the campus of Pittsburg State University and several of the cross country runners were known to have participated. On some nights the word would spread throughout the fraternities and sororities on campus that there might be some streaking that night in the quad. Several guys would show up in trench coats with nothing on underneath. They would quickly disrobe and run a short sprint in the nude.

However, that doesn't compare to the real streakers, the cross country team. The first known incident was when two or three masked runners ran through the Pittsburg, KS Mall. Not to be undone, Nixon and Doug Shreves went to the local watering hole, The Leather Ball on South Broadway Street one Saturday night. They told everyone to clear away from the bar. Then they ran around to the back door, burst in naked, jumped on the bar, and ran out the front door to the applause of dozens of patrons. If Coach Suenram knew about this he looked the other way since Nixon was an All-American.

In the fall semester of 1972, I was in an Art Appreciation class with Nixon. I remember the day when someone sneezed and he got up and walked out of the class because he did not want to catch their cold. The NAIA (National Association of Intercollegiate Athletics) Cross Country Championships were held on the campus of William Jewell College in Liberty, MO, in 1972. Coach Suenram drove us in a station wagon and when we went to pick up Nixon he was up in a tree for some unknown reason. When Coach said, "Hurry up, let's go." Mike jumped down and could have easily broken his ankle. We thought Coach Suenram was going to pass out.

I was blessed during my running career to have come across some outstanding runners who taught me what it is really like to be competitive. The first such runner was Mike Nixon. Mike lived on a small farm in Cherryvale, KS, which had been in his family for over 100 years. He spent his time hunting whatever was in season with a bow and arrow because it was more sporting than a shotgun. A few times Mike invited me to come home with him for the weekend and go hunting. Being from the city, I knew nothing about hunting, shooting a gun, or a bow and arrow. So, I would go along for the experience and watch Mike hunt.

Mike attended a small, rural high school in Altamont, KS, where I ended up teaching a few years later. He had not run any outstanding times in high school, but under the coaching of Dave Suenram and the high mileage that we ran, Mike blossomed. I only got to run with Mike for one year before he graduated, but I got to see him win the NAIA Cross Country Championships in 1972, place 2nd in the indoor two-mile run in 9:01, and 3rd in the 3000 meter steeplechase, and 6th in the three-mile run in the NAIA Outdoor Championships in 1973. What I remember most about Mike is that he constantly suffered from shin splints and always had his legs completely taped, yet he won nearly every race in record time. Since I was an early riser and loved to run as many miles as possible, I was asked to run six miles several mornings a week with Mike to better prepare him for his big races coming up. It was quite an honor for me. He was very humble and no one on campus knew just how good of a runner he was.

Mike ran his final race at the NAIA Outdoor National Track Championship in Arkadelphia, AR, on May 23, 1973. After he crossed the final line in the 3 mile run he took off his spikes, and said "That's it, I am done forever." To the best of my knowledge he never ran again. Sadly, he passed away at the young age of 51 with cancer.

Coach Dave Suenram summarized the 1972 cross country season by saying, "Leading the way throughout the year was All-American Mike Nixon, who won the National title with a time of 24:29.4 for five miles. The KSC thinclads also received strong support from Tyler Todd, Jim Scott, Randy Cook, Terry Cornelius, and Marcus Canipe."

In the spring of 1973, Coach Suenram planned for me to run in the NAIA College Marathon Championships in May at Arkadelphia, AR. So, he increased my mileage and entered Larry Grecian and me in the Groundhog Marathon in Morrilton, AR, on February 3, 1973. I ran two hours and 42 minutes and placed 4th behind "Gre" who ran 2:38:04

and got 2nd place. The winner was Terry Ziegler of Oklahoma University who ran 2:21:24. There were 50 finishers in the race.

On May 23, 1973, I set a PR in the NAIA College Marathon Championships. My time of two hours and 39 minutes put me in 10th place and barely missed earning All-American designation. In looking back at my training diary the two weeks leading up to this marathon I ran 110 and 108 miles. The winner was Lucien Rosa from Sri Lanka and Wisconsin-Parkside College who set a record in 2:26:01. Lucien had recently placed 4th in the Boston Marathon. In second place was Wayne Frongello from Boston State College in 2:29:29. Third place went to David Antogonoli from Edinboro State (PA) College in 2:30:43. Fourth place was Lionel Ortega from Adams State College in Colorado in 2:31:13. Fifth was Peter Frederickson from U.S. International College in California in 2:32:26. Sixth place and final All-American status went to David Slusser of Indiana College of Pennsylvania in 2:34:04.

Coach Suenram praised my effort in the marathon in the local newspaper by saying "Randy Cook ran in the 26 mile marathon and was in the middle of the 45-man field when he started to move up. He never quit, but kept plugging along and moved up to tenth at the finish line."

My diary also showed that the fall of 1973 was basically a disaster running wise. It seemed that I had one injury after another; mostly in the lower back and left thigh. I am thinking that the high mileage took its toll on me. I would rest it a few days then try to resume the normal hard workouts only to get injured again. In the 1970s it seems that the motto was "No Pain No Gain." I was sent to physical therapy at Mt. Carmel Hospital in Pittsburg, KS, where they used muscle stimulation, ice massage, whirlpool, ultra sound, stretching, and deep heat massages. I even resorted to swimming laps and jogging in the pool. I managed to run three cross country races in the fall of 1973, but the times were not outstanding. I was looking forward to being able to run pain free again soon. On December 1, 1973, I went to Topeka, KS, and set a PR in the Topeka Half Marathon in one hour and 16 minutes.

I came home to Norfolk for Christmas vacation and ran an eight mile race at the Naval Air Station. I was 3rd place overall and 1st in my age group in 46:44. The plan for the spring semester of 1974 was to run the NAIA National Marathon Championships again in May. My diary for the week of February 4-10 says that "I ran 80 miles this week and now feel strong enough and confident that I should be able to improve on my marathon time." On March 2, I had one of my most difficult days of running yet. In the morning I ran ten miles under 7:00 pace. Then at 2:00 pm I did a two-mile warm up followed by 20 by 440 yard laps on the track. Shot-putter Wally Autem timed me and I averaged 69.8 seconds with a 90 second rest in between. The next day I did a 15 mile run. I felt great! The problem with the spring semester is that I was doing my student teaching and had to commute 45 minutes one way so my mileage during the week was greatly reduced. I was trying to average 50 miles a week, but the bulk of it was on the weekends. Not a great way to prepare for an important marathon.

On May 5, 1974, I ran 12 miles hard in the morning; rested, then at 8:00 pm I did 30 X 440 yard runs on the track averaging 69.6 seconds with a 90 second rest in between each sprint. Teammate and National Champion shot putter Wally Autem graciously timed these intervals for me.

On May 23 I placed a disappointing 18th in the NAIA College Marathon Championships with a time of two hours and 44 minutes. I felt fine until about 16 miles then had to slow down for a lack of endurance. It was the same course as last year in Arkadelphia, AR, and the heat and humidity was the same as 1973 too. Lucien Rosa of Wisconsin-Parkside broke his own record and easily won the race. His time was 2:22:54 and broke the record of 2:26 that he set the previous year. In second place was Joe Catalano of Boston State College in 2:28:45. In third place was Curt Ankey from George Fox College in Oregon in 2:28:55. Wayne Aklyana from Claremont College in California was fourth in 2:30:49 and fifth was Roger Vann of John Brown University in Arkansas in 2:31:38. Thirty eight runners started the race, but several dropped out because of exhaustion and blisters.

On June 28, 1974, *"The Collegio,"* the student newspaper for Kansas State College of Pittsburg, did an article on me titled "Randy Cook runs 5,000 miles yearly." In the article I mentioned that "KSCP is fortunate to have one of the finest small college track teams in the country. Coach Suenram is an excellent distance runner's coach and he has the ability to get maximum effort out of each athlete." I will be forever grateful to Dave Suenram for his coaching expertise, making me a better runner, and helping me get started in my teaching and coaching career.

The first day of cross country practice was August 22, 1974, and we ran ten miles in the morning and another ten miles hard in the afternoon. This kind of mileage was typical for the fall of 1974. My weekly mileage for the next several weeks was 110, 108, 113, 95, 110, 100, 100, 107, 100, 140 (school record), and 72 as we "rested" for the cross country championships.

The Great Plains Athletic Conference Championship was held on our home course in Pittsburg, KS, on the golf course on November 2, 1974, in a down pour. It rained almost three inches in 30 minutes and runners were slipping and falling all over the place. I was extremely disappointed that I was beaten out by a teammate in a time trial for a position in the top seven just before the race so I could not run in the championships. However, the team won the championship so I was happy for the other runners and I could say that I was a member of the championship team. The Pittsburg State runners were Tyler Todd 1st, Dave Conover 2nd, Mark Rabuse 4th, Randy Latta 7th, Dave Savage 10th, Marvin Parker 12th, and Kent Neubert 20th place.

My last cross country race for Pittsburg State was on November 9, 1974, in Emporia, KS, for the Missouri Valley AAU Championships. In the cold rain I ran 28 minutes for five miles on a muddy course. It was a sad ending to the great times that I had running cross country in college. I don't think my heart was really in this race. We had already won the Conference Championship and in a few weeks I would be graduating and starting graduate school.

On December 20 I flew home to Norfolk for Christmas. The next day I ran the Seashore State Park 10 Mile Run in 57 minutes and got 2nd place behind Glenn Logan, the top local runner. I lost sight of him after the first mile when we went into the trails and I continually got lost, but still managed a good time.

A few of the memories of the Pittsburg State years include: the racing, jumping on, riding, then trying to jump off trains heading through Pittsburg as a way to get out of a few miles of running; "Camp Stockton" in the fall of 1972, when we had three workouts a day in the August heat while camping out with the mosquitoes; the 100 mile weeks of cross country season of 6 by 1 mile at Lincoln Park on Monday, six miles in the morning then 12-14 miles on Tuesday afternoon, ten miles for time on the golf course on Wednesday, six miles in the morning and 12-14 on Thursday afternoon, a "rest day" of six miles on Friday, race on Saturday, then a long run on Sunday. No wonder most of us in that generation stayed injured.

I cherish the friendships I made during my years at Pittsburg and I still keep in touch with Marcus Canipe, Jim Scott, Larry Grecian, Coach Suenram, and Dr. Elwyn Davis of the math department who ran with us, Terry Cornelius, Wally Autem, Dave Coen, and Dave Elliott.

47

Coach David L. Suenram had this to say about my running career at Pittsburg State University. "Randy Cook was part of a dedicated, talented, and spirited group of distance and middle-distance runners that represented Pittsburg State University, in the early to mid 1970s. They won the first Conference and District Cross Country Championships in the school's history. I remember Randy best for his everyday hard work ethic, loyalty, and commitment to the cross country and track and field program. This commitment extends to the present and is exemplified by his generosity to the program." He added, "I was privileged to have been Randy's coach."

Mike Nixon passed away on February 24, 2002 in Joplin, MO where he had been undergoing treatment. Teammate Marcus Canipe attended the funeral on March 1, and described the events of that day. Marcus said that if we had to describe a "Mike Nixon kind of day and place," you might picture a gray sky, temperatures just above freezing, a stiff wind off the plains, and an occasional rain—the kind of day Mike would put on a long sleeved t-shirt and shorts, and maybe some light cotton gloves or socks on his hands, a stocking cap, and then he'd head out for a nice long run, loving every minute of it. "

"If you can picture him running on the "marathon course," a flat gravel sectional road a couple miles from town with a train track intersecting the roads, then you'd have a clear picture of Mike's final resting place. It struck me as a "Mike Nixon kind of day and place."

In October 2001 I returned to Pittsburg, KS for the

Homecoming celebration. I asked my host, Elwyn Davis, if he would mind driving us to see Nixon's grave site. As we made the ninety minute drive, we passed Independence, KS where Laura Ingalls Wilder lived at one time and got the inspiration for Little House on the Prairie.

You could close your eyes and imagine buffalo roaming these very lands and settlers crossing what are now two lane roads, in covered wagons. When we arrived at the cemetery I was surprised at how wide open the view is. Kansas is very flat in that part of the state. The wind was blowing with no trees in sight to slow it down that day much as the day of Nixon's funeral that Marcus described.

Although I only ran on the team for one year with Mike, he meant a lot to me. We were about the same age and older than the freshmen and sophomores on the team. I wish I lived closer and was able to attend the funeral.

I greatly appreciate Marcus for keeping the teammates informed of Mike's passing.

I Am a Teacher Now
Chapter 5
1975 – 1978

"Do not go where the path may lead,
go instead where there is no path and leave a trail."

Ralph Waldo Emerson

I graduated with my bachelor's degree in Health and Physical Education in December 1974, and started graduate school in the spring semester of 1975. I received a Graduate Assistantship to help coach the track team and to teach some handball/racquetball classes. I was grateful for this opportunity, but coaching the sprinters was not as exciting as coaching or running with my distance buddies. I owe so much to Coach Suenram for all that he taught me about running and coaching. I knew that I wanted to become a track coach and teacher shortly after I arrived in Pittsburg. My best friend on the track team, Wally Autem, was a shot putter and discus thrower and he taught those techniques to me. I learned as much as possible about every event because I just had the feeling that I would be a coach someday. Coach Suenram also spent a lot of time preparing me to be a coach and even helped get me a job at Liberal High School in Liberal, MO in the fall of 1975.

While I was home in Norfolk on Christmas break, I won an eight mile race at the Naval Air Station in 43:14. A few days later I was running in downtown Norfolk, VA, along The Hague, when I saw two runners ahead of me, so I ran hard to catch up to them. They were Dr. David Young and Dr. Rudi Schuster who were running on their lunch break. I stopped to talk to them and introduced myself and said that I was home on vacation. They told me about a new running club being formed in the area named the Tidewater Striders. I got an application from them, sent in my dues and became one of the original members. Little did I know that 35 years later I would be elected to the Tidewater Striders Hall of Fame. Dr. Schuster became my family doctor and Dr. Young became my orthopedic surgeon when I moved back to Norfolk, VA, in June 1978. Dr. Young eventually operated on my left foot and right hip joint and gave me untold number of cortisone shots in my feet and knees for pain.

When I returned to Pittsburg, KS, for the spring semester of 1975, I started graduate school so my running took a back seat. My weekly mileage during the spring and summer was between 40 – 60 miles per week, which wasn't bad considering I was taking a heavy load of classes and coaching; but not enough to prepare for a marathon.

On September 1, 1975, I drove to Columbia, MO with Dick Carr and Wally Wood for the Heart of America Marathon. This was my 11th marathon. The race started at 6 am to avoid the heat, but it was still 75 degrees at the start. It was dark when we started and I knew nothing about the course and how hilly it was, so I just tried to keep the leaders in sight. After six miles I found myself in the lead as the other runners slowed their pace. I eventually had a lead of almost three minutes at the half way point and thought I was cruising to a victory, but it was not to be. I was caught and passed just past the 25 mile mark by Tim Hendricks of Omaha, NE. I still ran two hours and 39 minutes for 2nd place overall, but since I was the first finisher from Kansas or Missouri, I was the Missouri Valley Champion. My time was the 5th fastest in the history of the race and Tim's time was 4th fastest. Hendricks was a very worthy winner. I later learned that he had won this race five times in the past seven years. He knew the course like the back of his hand and where the steep hills were and the best place to make his move. I obviously went out too fast for the heat and humidity and paid the price at the end. I was told that this is one of the most difficult marathon courses in the United States and that my time would equate to a sub 2:30 time on a flat course. Wally Wood ran 3:14 for 29th place and Dick Carr 4:33 for 70th place. A total of 96 runners from 11 states started the race and seventy eight finished.

I was planning on running the Tri States Marathon again in Falls City, NE, on October 18 but it wasn't to be. I filled up my Plymouth Duster with gas and picked up Wally Wood, a graduate student in Pittsburg, and started the trip. We got about 30 miles before we were hit head on by a farmer coming towards us in our lane as we crested a hill. My car was totaled and Wally busted his head open when he hit the windshield. I hurt my right arm on the steering wheel and right knee on the console. Wally and I spent some time in the emergency room before Elwyn Davis came from Pittsburg and took us home. My knee hurt for several weeks and my arm was in a sling, but it could have been much worse. When I got the insurance money from the accident, I bought another Plymouth Duster. That car was like a tank and saved my life.

On November 30, 1975, I eased back into racing with a win in a four mile race in Carthage, MO, in 22:08 and on December 20 I won a ten mile race in Chanute, KS, in 55:27.

1976 started well when I won the eight mile race at the Naval Air Station in Norfolk, VA, in 45 minutes, while home for Christmas vacation. On January 25 I won a hilly five mile race in Carthage, MO, and on February 15, I placed 3rd overall in a 15 mile race from Sarcoxie to Carthage, MO, and on March 7, I won a 10 mile race in Liberal, MO, in 56 minutes.

I completed my Master's Degree in Health and Physical Education at Pittsburg State University in July 1976. I am proud that I completed my advanced degree in one semester and two summers. I needed a break from the hard work of studying, so I drove to Norfolk with Mark Rabuse, an All American teammate at Pittsburg State. In the three weeks that we were in Virginia, we took advantage of the Tidewater Striders Summer Track Series held every Tuesday night at Kempsville High School in Virginia Beach and ran some road races on the weekends. I enjoyed playing tour guide and showing Mark all of the historic sights of Jamestown, Yorktown and Williamsburg.

As we drove back to Kansas, Mark and I stopped in Washington, D.C. to tour the city. We ran about eight miles running from monument to monument, the White House, and the Capitol, posing for pictures along the way. It was a great way to see the city. We then jumped in the car and drove to Ohio for the night. You can do those things when you are young. However, now I get tired just driving the four hours to Washington, D.C.!

I started my new job in August of 1976 in Altamont, KS, at Labette County High School, teaching U.S. History, and Health and Physical Education. I also coached the offensive line on the varsity football team, junior varsity basketball, and high school track. All this for the huge sum of $8,000. The football players loved having a hefty 145 pound runner on the blocking sled. They could push me to the next county if they had wanted to.

Since Altamont, KS, was close to Oklahoma, I started racing more in places like Bartlesville and Tulsa. On September 11, 1976, I placed 2nd in a six mile run in Bartlesville, OK, in 34 minutes. On October 17 I ran my 12th marathon, the Tri States Marathon in Nebraska. My time of two hours and 49 minutes was only good enough for 15th place. I ran a 5K in Tulsa on November 13 in 16:40 and got 2nd place overall.

In the spring of 1977, several members of the track team that I coached at Labette County High School in Altamont, KS did well in the State High School Championships. Terry Gossard was 3rd place in the 60 yard dash and 6th in the 100 yard dash. Ron McMunn was 6th in the javelin and the 880 yard relay team of Randy Eisenbart, Terry Gossard, Mike McCoach, and Calvin Schnoebelin was 5th in the state. I still keep in touch with these guys even though I live hundreds of miles away.

Marcus Canipe, Jim Scott, and I were instrumental in forming a new running team for post graduate college runners and called ourselves "Club Midwest." Jim took the initiative and had racing shirts printed up at a sporting goods store in Kansas City. We hosted our first race, an eight mile run in Pittsburg, KS, on December 12, 1976. Jim Scott won in 40 minutes and I was 8th in 43 minutes, a new PR.

I started the New Year by winning the Tulsa Running Club's 5K race in Mohawk Park, in 16:27 and on January 23, 1977, I won a five mile race in Carthage, MO. I won again on February 11th, this time a 15 mile race from Sarcoxie to Carthage, MO in a PR of one hour and 27 minutes. On February 19 I ran 33 minutes for a 10K in the South East Kansas Heart Run in Pittsburg, KS. The Tulsa Running Club hosted another 5K on April 9, 1977, and I placed 2nd in a PR of 16:20.

I spent most of the summer of 1977 at home in Norfolk, to be close to my dad since his health had declined. I started to dedicate my training and racing to my father who was in the early stages of cancer. My father would live for four more years, but it was difficult to see him those last few years. Dad was a barber all of his working life, standing long hours every day. He had poor circulation in his legs and had surgery in the 1970s to have the veins stripped from his legs. I figured that if dad could somehow still stand and cut hair then I could use my legs to run. He was a fighter and never complained about the pain he was having, so I felt that I needed to be as tough as he was. I was not blessed with pure speed, but I made the most of what talent and endurance that I had and I was not going to be outworked.

I heard that the Tidewater Striders Running Club and the Norfolk Recreation Bureau were sponsoring a 24 hour relay at Old Dominion University from June 17-18, 1977. I went to the track to see what it was all about. The rules were that there could be up to ten members on a team who would each run a mile then pass the baton to the next runner in line until all ten runners have run. This relay keeps going for 24 hours and you see how many miles your team can cover. I was not on a team, but I was extremely lucky that a team comprised of runners from Virginia Tech and East Carolina University needed one more runner and I was asked to join them.

The relay race started at 6:00 pm on a Friday evening and ended at 6:00 pm the next day. We drew straws to determine the order that we would run in. It was decided that we would try to break the state record of 253 miles. We would stretch and jog a little before it was our turn to run again to be able to run as fast as possible. One of the members of the U.S. Marines team said "You guys will never make it at that pace." That just gave us more of an incentive. There were four other teams in the competition. A few members of my team tried to see how many miles they could run under 5:00 per mile pace. Robbie White, a former star at Norfolk Catholic High School, had to stop about 3:00 am. He had worked a construction job in the 100 degree heat all day and simply ran out of gas. Steve Sawyer, formerly of Kempsville High School in Virginia Beach, dropped out about 7:00 am. The rules state that if a runner drops out they cannot be replaced, so we were down to eight runners trying to break the record in the scorching heat of June.

The temperature rose to 100 degrees again on the second day. We covered a state record 261 miles in 24 hours! I ran 28 miles and averaged 5:33 per mile. As team member Harold Goldsberry said, "This is worse than a marathon! At least you can eat in a marathon. Out here, you can't eat and you can't sleep." We had the assistance of Harold's parents as our unofficial time keepers and my father, Clyde Cook, brought a transistor radio and snacks and kept us company during part of the long night. When my dad got out of his car and limped to our team tent, it brought tears to my eyes and there was no way I was going to drop out.

In a Tidewater Striders Summer Track meet on July 12, I ran the mile in 4:46 and 2 mile in 10:06. I was still averaging 50-60 miles a week and had not missed a day of running in over a year.

On September 3 I was 5th place overall in a 15K in Tulsa in a PR of 51:07 and on October 8 I ran a PR for the two mile in 9:57 in Tulsa.

I went to Tulsa again on October 29 for the AAU men's 20K National Championships. I ran 1:11:15 for 21st place and my Tulsa Running Club team finished 2nd to the

Greater Boston Track Club. The race was won by Gary Tuttle of California, followed by Dick Mahoney of Massachusetts, George Mason of Kansas, Vincent Fleming of Massachusetts, and Mark Duggan of Massachusetts. A total of 92 started the grueling race and 83 finished. It was 82 degrees with very high humidity and a bright sun that made it tough on the runners.

For Thanksgiving of 1977, I went to Cameron, MO, with running friend Elwyn Davis and his family. We ran ten miles at 6:20 pace in 26 degree temperature in the snow and ice on the morning of Thanksgiving Day. Soon after the run I became sick and was unable to eat Thanksgiving dinner with his wonderful family. I stayed in bed all that day and night with the flu, but still ran four miles the next day to keep my running streak alive. I had run for 384 consecutive days and, despite the 16 degrees temperature outside and running a fever, I HAD to keep my streak going!

In 1977, I ran 3,016 miles for an average of 58 miles per week.

1978 started out well for me. On January 7 I won a five mile race in Carthage, MO and a 15 mile race on February 5, from Sarcoxie to Carthage on a hilly course in Missouri. On February 18 I won the SE Kansas Heart Run 10K and a week later I won my age group in the Tulsa 30K in a PR of one hour and 47 minutes.

When the school year ended in May, I resigned from my teaching and coaching positions at Labette County High

School and moved to Norfolk and started looking for a teaching/ coaching job. My dad's health was worse and his cancer was more important than what I would do for money at the time. I applied for teaching jobs in several local cities and would be a substitute teacher, if necessary, to make ends meet. Thankfully my parents allowed me to live with them to save money.

I was very fortunate that the Tidewater Striders are one of the best running clubs in the United States and have road races nearly every weekend plus track meets on Tuesday nights.

One of the highlights of the summer of 1978 include running the 5K in 16:01 on June 8 in the Virginia AAU Senior Track & Field Meet in Richmond, VA, and getting 4th place in the state.

On July 1 the Tidewater Striders Running Club hosted the Road Runners Club of America National Postal Championship One Hour Run on the track. The event was held at Manor High School in Portsmouth, VA. The object is to see how many miles you can run in exactly 60 minutes. Race director, Charlie George submitted my distance to RRCA national headquarters. I soon found out that I had the 4th best result in the United States. I ran ten miles and 1553 yards.

On July 15, I went to Charlottesville, VA, for the Virginia AAU Masters State Championships. I won the 1500m in 4:24, the 5K in 16:41, and 10K in 34:51 all in the same day and with little rest in between.

In the middle of August 1978 I finally got hired to teach U.S. History and World Geography at Granby High School in Norfolk, VA. I heard about an opening for a cross country coach at Virginia Wesleyan College in Norfolk. I applied and got the job just before school started, but did not have time to recruit any runners. Fortunately, I had enough runners to field a team and senior Gary Cummisk won the Conference Championship.

My consecutive days of running ended at 652 days on August 21, 1978, when I got pneumonia. I was running sprints on a golf course in the 90 degree heat when I realized I was late for an appointment. I jumped in the car without cooling down and turned the air conditioner on high. The next thing I knew I was sneezing, coughing, and hacking. I missed two weeks of running and the first week of my new teaching job.

On November 12 I ran the Northwest River Park 30K in one hour and 47 minutes getting 2nd place behind William and Mary runner Craig Allen. I beat future Tidewater Striders Hall of Famer Pete Gibson who was 3rd place.

Pete Gibson is a few years younger than me and over the years we always had some battles when we ran. One of my favorite race photos is when Pete and I are sprinting side by side at the end of a half-marathon in Seashore State Park. Out of mutual respect for each other, we decided to hold hands at the finish line which signifies that we wanted to tie. We ran 1:11:32 for the 13.1 miles then flipped a coin to see who got the first place trophy. Pete is one of the nicest people you could ever hope to meet, yet one of the most competitive that I have had the pleasure to run against. If I beat Pete in a race, I knew that I had a good day and if he beat me, I did not feel bad at all. When the Tidewater Striders Hall of Fame was founded, I quickly nominated Pete Gibson and he was unanimously selected by the Hall of Fame committee.

I badly wanted to win the Virginia State Masters 10K Cross Country Championships on November 18, in Newport News. I ran beside my nemesis and future Peninsula Track Club and Tidewater Striders Hall of Famer, Lew Faxon, the entire race, but he out kicked me at the finish line. I ran 34:27 on a muddy course and was 2nd in the state for all 30-39 year olds.

Lew Faxon is a few years older than me and was the grittiest, fiercest, most determined runner I have ever seen. He won many races, state championships, and even National Championships on guts. Lew reminds me of one of my heroes, Steve Prefontaine, who ran for the University of Oregon. He ran as hard as he could for as long as he could and if someone beat him they would have to pay a steep price.

On Thanksgiving Day, November 23, I ran the inaugural Turkey Trot 10K in 32:37 at Mt. Trashmore in Virginia Beach. I only got 7th place, but lost to top college runners. Finn Pincus from the University of Virginia won in 30:32, followed by Robbie White from Virginia Tech, then Barry Heath representing the Royal British Navy.

In 1978, I ran 3,263 miles or about 63 miles per week.

Chapter 6
We're Not in Kansas Anymore
1979 – 1980

"You train best where you are the happiest."

Frank Shorter

My first race of 1979 was the Boardwalk 5-Mile in Virginia Beach on January 6th. In spite of the frigid temperatures and strong winds I set a personal record for a five mile road race in 26:16 and finished 3rd overall. The winner was Finn Pincus, a former runner for the University of Virginia and 2nd place was Ken Lampert a former runner from Virginia Tech.

On January 13th I ran the North Carolina Half-Marathon Championships in Bethel, NC. My time was 1:11:47 for a personal record for this distance. I was 3rd overall and 1st in my age division. Bethel is a small town in southeastern North Carolina in peanut country. I have no idea why Bethel would be awarded the half-marathon championships because there is absolutely nothing there except very long stretches of flat deserted roads. They must have been the only town or city that applied to have the race. We started and finished at a local church in town then headed out on the two lane country roads. The course was out and back so it was easy for the course marshals to keep track of the runners. The race officials only had to check off the runners as they made the turn around. When we crossed the finish line at the church the members had prepared a nice treat of hot soup, rolls, coffee and tea. It was well appreciated after running in the cold January temperature.

I upped my mileage to 70-80 a week, but was having persistent pains in my left knee and left thigh. Instead of backing off my training or taking a rest I continued to train hard because there were so many races on the horizon that I wanted to run and do well in. Why anyone would subject themselves to this punishment I don't know. Well, I do know, but that doesn't make it right. I was 31 years old and thought I was bulletproof and that any injury was just a minor setback. All runners live for the "now," not thinking of running 30 years in the future. All highly competitive runners feel that they have worked too hard to get in top condition to take rest days. You know that your competitors are working hard and you don't want them to get an edge on you. Also, running is addictive in a good way and if a runner has to miss a few days due to injuries they feel guilty. If you have to miss more than just a couple of days of running then a runner starts to gets depressed. Just imagine how I felt when I was unable to run for 25 years!

In February of 1979, I ran the Yorktown, VA, 15 Miler in one hour and 27 minutes. I was the 4th place runner behind Robbie Pecht from the University of Virginia, Craig Allen, formerly of William and Mary, and Lew Faxon, a future Tidewater Striders Hall of Famer. The roads were covered in ice and snow, but there were still over 100 runners despite the 21 degree temperature.

Two weeks later, I turned the tables and beat my good friend Craig Allen at the Athletic Attic 10K in Virginia

Beach in 32:28. The race finished at the top of Mt. Trashmore and I somehow found the strength to hold off Craig by two seconds. Barry Heath, an officer in the British Royal Navy, won the race in 31:22 followed by Jack Nash in 31:55. Stanley Olszewski was 3rd in 32:15, David Raunig 4th in 32:20 and I was 5th place. The race went around Mt. Trashmore, a huge landfill packed down then planted with grass to make it look natural. There is a paved road to the top on one side for soapbox derby races, a skateboard ramp, playground, picnic tables, and man-made lake with boat rentals. Since this is the only hill in Virginia Beach, the local high school teams often train here and run their cross country meets on the property.

Athletic Attic is a chain of running stores that was started by Jimmy Carnes, the coach of the University of Florida and Florida Track Club runner Marty Liquori in 1973. At its peak they owned 165 stores. In addition to teaching, coaching my high school track team after school I worked at the Athletic Attic store in Virginia Beach on weekends. I was given the opportunity to manage a new store in Greenville, NC, but turned it down for the security of a teaching position.

I felt that I was ready to run well since I was doing some intense workouts. My favorite speed workouts were 20 by 220 yard sprints, 5 by one mile runs at 5:00 per mile, and 10 by 440 yard sprints to the top of the Hampton Boulevard Bridge in Norfolk. I looked forward to meeting Greg Eck and Craig Allen every Sunday morning at Seashore State Park in Virginia Beach for long runs between 14 to 20 miles. I knew I was in great condition for a marathon when we ran these distances in less than 6:30 per mile and it seemed so easy.

Seashore State Park, now called First Landing State Park, recognized the fact that Captain John Smith and his crew landed at this spot and planted a cross before deciding to head further west up the James River and founded a settlement they named Jamestown or the Towne of James after King James of England. It is the best kept secret in the Tidewater area. There are dozens of miles of wooded trails with Spanish moss hanging from the trees that make it seem as if you were in a movie set. As soon as you start running on some of the back trails, you can close your eyes and envision Native Americans roaming the area.

On March 10 I ran the AAU State Masters Indoor Championships in Lexington, VA. I ran the 1500 meters in 4:27 and the 5K in 16:12 on the same day.

The Shamrock 5 Mile was held on March 17 and I was the 4th place runner. My time of 26:11 was a new personal record for five miles. The three runners ahead of me were Richard Ferguson in 25:27, Ken Lampert from Virginia Tech in 25:48, and Ray McDaniels from Virginia Tech in 26:06.

I ran the Colonial Relays Half Marathon in Williamsburg, VA, on April 8 and ran 1:11:53 for the 13.1 mile race. I was 6th place overall and first in the 30-39 age division. The race was won by Guy Crane from Virginia Tech in 1:09:16. Guy was running 140 miles per week in an attempt to run a marathon fast enough to qualify for the Olympic Marathon trials.

On April 22 I was 5th place overall in the Azalea Festival 10K in 32:56. On April 27, I did a workout of 4 by 440 @ 68 seconds with a 60 second rest then 8 by 220 in 33 seconds with a 30 seconds rest. Surprise, surprise my left leg hurt the next day so I had to back off my training.

I was first place in the 30-39 age division in the Elizabeth River Run in 34 minutes on May 12. Although I won my age division, I was not satisfied with my time and I knew something wasn't right with my leg. I tried to run the next day, but the pain was too severe. I went back to Dr. Young on May 24 and was diagnosed with a stress fracture. I ended up missing four weeks of running. Needless to say, I wasn't very pleasant to be around. Hopefully this was just a bump in the road and I would come back stronger after the forced rest.

I resumed training the end of May and ran 35-60 miles a week the next four weeks. On June 30 I got 2nd place behind Lew Faxon in the 5K in 16:42 and I won the 10K in 35 minutes on the track in Charlottesville, VA, in the AAU State Masters Championships. Faxon set a record for 30 year olds in 15:56 for the 5K on the track. The weather was hot and humid and the start of the 10K was delayed because of a downpour. When the rain stopped, the track was saturated with several puddles that we had to run through. Most of the runners ran shirtless because it was so hot and steamy.

Someone had the brilliant idea to have a 10K on a Sunday afternoon in the middle of July. The Wakefield, VA Shady Run on July 15 was run in 95 degree heat. 290 brave souls showed up for the race and only 11 dropped out. It was named the "Shady Run" because there were a few trees along the course, but they didn't help lower the temperature at all. I managed to run 33:55 which was 1st in the 30-34 age division. I was 4th place overall behind Craig Allen, Stan Olszewski, and Richard Ferguson from Virginia Tech. I was very happy that I beat my old nemesis Lew Faxon.

In the Tidewater Striders Summer Track Series I ran the mile in 4:42 and 2 mile in 10:02 on the track on the same night. I just could not get under 4:40 for the mile. Maybe if I cut my mileage in half and did nothing but speed work I could have broken that magical 4:40 barrier, but I was better at the longer distances so I just continued to run long and hard and do the best I could at the shorter distances.

On August 11 I ran 16:06 in the Portsmouth City Park 5K Run. My time was only good enough for 16th overall, but I did win my age group (30-34). The times were much faster in those days. Race director Winston Brown used all of his contacts to get the best runners from every local city to come and run his race. I think runners today would think I was crazy if I told them that 15 runners ran faster than 16:00 for a 5K in Tidewater, VA, in 1979. Many races are now won by men running 17:00 minutes and slower.

In looking at my running log during this time frame, I admit that I was consumed with running. I was running 10-

12 workouts a week, which meant that I often ran eight miles at 5:30 am at 6:30 pace or faster and did the main workout that afternoon. On Sundays I typically did a long run of 12-15 miles at Seashore State Park. I increased this distance up to 20 miles when preparing for the marathon. I was running races three-four times a month and running two hard workouts a week so I never gave my body a chance to rest.

During the late seventies and eighties there was a running category for couples. I participated in many of these races with my wife, Carolyn. On September 28, we earned the title of the fastest married couple in the area at the Midnight Couples Run 5K in Virginia Beach. I was the second overall finisher in 16:14 and Carolyn ran 20:15. Our combined time of 36:29 beat the next fastest couple by three minutes.

I went back to see Dr. David Young on October 12, this time for my right shin. He gave me a prescription of Butazolidin and said I have peristitis in the leg. So what did I do? I took one day off then resumed hard training. I had an important race coming up so I could not afford to take time off and rest it.

I ended 1979 by winning the Virginia AAU 10K Masters Cross Country Championships in 34:07 on November 17. I ran 3,497 miles in 1979 or about 67 miles per week.

Chapter 7
Setting Lofty Goals
1980

*"Let me tell you the secret that has led me to my goal.
My strength lies solely in my tenacity."*

Louis Pasteur

My right leg hurt so bad that I was forced to take another week off from January 14-20 of 1980. When I resumed training the next week, I ran 54 miles. The following weeks I ran 75, 71, and 77 miles. This probably wasn't the smartest thing to do if I wanted to get well.

I ran the Yorktown Battlefield 15 Mile on February 17 in one hour and 25 minutes for a personal record for 15 miles. I finished in 2nd place behind my good friend Craig Allen. Craig kicked butt that day beating me by over three minutes. I did beat Lew Faxon, that tough competitor from Hampton, VA. Carolyn was the first place female in 1:45:38.

On February 24 I was the race director for the Athletic Attic 10K in Virginia Beach. Since Jimmy Carnes was the owner of all of the Athletic Attic stores and also the track coach for the 1980 Olympic Team, the local owners, George and Patty Wagner, invited me to go to New York City the following weekend for the National Indoor Track and Field Championships. They wanted to present a check to Carnes and the US Olympic Team from the race proceeds. I jumped at the chance!

69

The track meet was at Madison Square Garden, two blocks away from our hotel. We stayed at the Statler Hilton, ate at Tavern on the Green and Gallagher's Steakhouse, saw the Broadway play "Ain't Misbehavin," and attended the track meet. The mood was rather somber, especially for the athletes because President Carter declared that the United States might be boycotting the 1980 Olympics since the Soviet Union had recently invaded Afghanistan. I got autographs from most of the top athletes that weekend including Joan Benoit, Eamonn Coghlan from Ireland, Dwight Stones, and Louise Ritter.

As we left New York on Sunday morning March 2 it started to snow very lightly. As we drove through Delaware and the Eastern Shore of Maryland, the snow started coming down harder. We had about 100 miles to drive on Route 13 before crossing the Chesapeake Bay Bridge Tunnel. We started to realize that we had not seen any cars coming towards us for several miles.

Could the weather be bad on the other side of the bridge in Virginia Beach? Should we pull over and stop at a motel?

We decided to keep going because there was no snow on the bridges going towards Virginia Beach. However, as soon as we exited the bridge and got onto Northampton Boulevard in Virginia Beach, the snow was up to the car doors and we were stuck. The Virginia Department of Transportation should have closed the Chesapeake Bay Bridge Tunnel and not allowed us to cross.

We were stuck dead in our tracks and other drivers began abandoning their cars. Mr. and Mrs. Wagner called their son to rescue us with his Jeep. They allowed me to stay at their Virginia Beach home. It took three days before I was able to get to my house in Norfolk, 20 miles away.

The Ringling Brothers Circus was in the middle of a performance at the Scope Arena in downtown Norfolk when the snow storm hit. There were 2,300 people in attendance who were forced to spend the night in the arena. It snowed again the next winter when the circus arrived, so it became a standing joke for a few years that there would be another blizzard whenever the circus came to town.

In March of 1980 I ran a 5K in 16:39 and the 1500 meters in 4:33 in the AAU Masters State Indoor Championships in Lexington, VA.

In April, I ran the Colonial Relays Half Marathon in Williamsburg, VA, in 1:13:29 for 8th place overall and 1st in the 30-39 age division. I was satisfied with the time since it was such a hilly course.

I was the overall winner of the Azalea Festival 10K in Norfolk, on April 19. I was presented with a beautiful autographed photograph of Queen Azalea, Monique Hamilius from Luxembourg, giving me the trophy. My wife was the first place female in this race. When our daughter, Jennifer, was born in January of 1981 we hoped that she would grow up to be a runner, but it wasn't to be. She certainly had the genes for it.

On April 27 I went to Raleigh, NC, for the South East U.S. Masters Track & Field Championships. I ran the 10K in 34:05 and got 2nd place in the 30-34 age division.

On May 10, 1980, I ran the Elizabeth River Run in Norfolk in 33:08 and got 14th place overall and 2nd in the 30-34 age group and on May 24 the Yorktown Victory Run 8-Mile in 43:35 for 5th place overall and 1st place in the 30-39 age division.

I ran several races in June of 1980. On June 7, I ran a 5K at Granby High School in 16:24 and got 3rd place overall and first in the 30-39 age division. On June 14, the St. Judes 5K was run in Virginia Beach and my time was 16:00 for a personal record. Later that month, I ran the half mile in 2:14 and the two mile run in 10:04 at the Tidewater Striders Summer Track Series in Virginia Beach. Finally, I went to Charlottesville for the Virginia AAU State Masters Track & Field Championships. In 95 degree heat, I ran the 5K in 16:28, 10K in 33:57, and the 1500 meters in 4:29 in the same day.

I continued to run 80-90 miles a week in July and still run a race almost every weekend, do a long run on Sunday, and at least one hard sprint workout per week. My best races for July 1980 were the one mile run in 4:42 and winning the 5K in 16:04 in the Portsmouth, VA, Freedom Run.

In August of 1980 I set another personal record of 37:46 in the 7.2 mile race around the Mariner's Museum in Newport News, VA. I also ran the 5K in 16:02 in the

Portsmouth, VA, City Park Run, and then set another personal record for the 5K on August 30 in 15:53 at the Virginia Association for Blind Athletes race in Norfolk, VA. This was while running 85-100 miles a week. I was feeling great and there were no injuries at the moment.

I ran 80 – 100 miles a week for the remainder of 1980, stayed relatively healthy and my times continued to improve. My next goal was the Shamrock Marathon in March 1981. Coach Roy Chernock of the College of William and Mary agreed to coach me. He would send me workouts then discuss my progress each weekend. Roy had me convinced that I was capable of running a marathon under two hours and 30 minutes. I needed a coach and motivator to direct me in the right direction to attain this goal and Coach Chernock was very gracious to help me. When the time came for Shamrock in March, I was going to run my heart out for him!

My races for September 1980 were: the Ft. Story 10K Run (Virginia Beach) where I ran 32:56 on a very hilly course. My time placed me 10th overall and 1st in the 30-34 age group. On September 19, I ran a 5K in 16:15 for the Tidewater Striders Couples Run on the Virginia Beach Boardwalk. My last race in September was the Virginia Ten Miler in Lynchburg, VA. I ran 54:40 and got 3rd place in the 30-34 age division.

There were several major races that I chose to run in November of 1980. On November 1, I ran the Elizabeth City, NC, 10K in 32:54. I was 2nd place overall and 1st in the 30-39 age division. My next race was the Tidewater

Striders 15K at Northwest River Park in Chesapeake in 50:40 which was another PR. On November 15, 1980, I won the Virginia AAU Masters 10K State Cross Country Championships at Mt. Trashmore in Virginia Beach. My time was 33:33. I ran another 10K on November 23 the Chesapeake Challenge in 32:44 and the Turkey Trot on November 27. My time for the Turkey Trot was 33:26 and I was 3rd place overall.

1980 ended with two major races. On December 14 I tied for 2nd place with Cletus Griffin in the Tidewater Striders 20K in a PR of 67:55.

My final race of 1980 was the Nature Trail ten mile run on December 27 in Seashore State Park. Alberto Salazar had just won the New York Marathon in October and set a course record in 2:09 for the 26.2 mile race. He slipped into town without any fanfare just to visit his brother Rick, who was stationed in Virginia Beach, in the U.S. Navy. It was a bitter cold day with the temperature in the low 30s with sleet during the entire race. Alberto wore cotton sweat pants and an old hooded sweatshirt and just ran the race as a workout. His winning time was 51:07, followed by top local runner Harry Freeman in 52:48 and I was 3rd in 54:26. I beat Rick Salazar who was 4th in 55:42.

In 1980, I ran 4250 miles for an average of almost 82 miles per week.

NAIA Marathon 1974

1980 Virginia State Championship

1983 Shamrock Marathon

2013 YMCA Run

Chapter 8
My Dream Marathon
1981

*"The will to win means nothing
without the will to prepare."*

Juma Ikangaa

I had one big goal in 1981, the Shamrock Marathon on March 14. I was also eagerly anticipating the birth of my daughter, Jennifer. She was born on January 13, 1981, just past midnight in DePaul Hospital in Norfolk. Three days after Jenny was born I was honored to receive the Tidewater Striders Achievement Award for Submasters (30-39 year olds).

The weeks leading up to the Shamrock Marathon I ran the following miles per week: 108, 90, 99, 97, 72, 89, 93, 104, 110 and 89. Coach Roy Chernock from William & Mary was still coaching me and I felt capable of running a good time if I could just stay healthy for the next two and a half months.

On January 10 I won the Tidewater Striders 25K in a PR of 1:30:53 and on January 18 I won the Peninsula Track Club's 10.8 mile championship in 58:09.

In February, I finished in 3rd place for the Tidewater Striders 30K run behind future Tidewater Striders Hall of Famer, Dave McDonald and Craig Allen. My time of 1:45:38 was another personal record. On February 15 I won the Yorktown Battlefield 15 Miler in 1:22:31. I was ready for Shamrock!

March 14, 1981 finally arrived, but it was cold with a strong wind out of the north that would be in our faces the last five miles. This is the race that all of my training was geared for. I had done all of the preparation including the 20 mile runs on Sunday mornings at Seashore State Park, the 5:30 am runs in the dark and cold winter mornings, the speed work, and hill workouts. I got a good night's sleep and felt ready to go.

When the starter's pistol was shot by race director Jerry Bocrie, I tried to maintain a steady pace. The first five miles on Atlantic Avenue, in Virginia Beach was directly into a 30 mile an hour wind with gusts up to 40 miles an hour. I knew after months of training and racing distances from the 15K up to the 30K that I was capable of running a pace of about 5:40 per mile. Coach Chernock convinced me that I could run two hours and 30 minutes or less if I ran intelligently. I had the times for each mile written on a piece of paper tucked into my Casio watch band. This is how we used to have to do it before there were Garmin GPS watches.

Despite the strong wind and trying to "hold back," my first mile was 5:25. I said to myself, "What have I done? I am going to blow this race in the first mile." I eased off the throttle and began to run my own race and not worry about trying to keep up with the leaders.

There were several runners capable of running faster

than two hours and 20 minutes ahead of me so I had no business being with them. Just past mile five, we turned left at 64th Street then entered Seashore State Park, my old stomping grounds.

We then had to run three and a half miles on the sandy, muddy trails, but at least we were sheltered from the wind by the trees. When we exited the park, we ran on Shore Drive for a half-mile before turning into Fort Story Army Base.

Now we had the strong wind at our backs as we started heading south. I held back to keep my form and stay on pace, but there were runners literally flying by me. I was hoping that I would catch some of them later since we still had about 15 miles to go. All the way down the boardwalk the wind was pushing me, but I knew that I would have to run into the teeth of the wind when we turned for home.

After we left the boardwalk, we crossed the Rudee Inlet Bridge and headed south for a mile until we turned into Camp Pendleton Army Base. After running two miles on Camp Pendleton, we made a right hand turn and started heading north on General Booth Boulevard, directly into the 30 mile per hour wind.

At this time I was running next to George Keim from Toronto, Canada and we made a pact to take turns breaking the wind about every two minutes. George and I were able to make this work for only about one mile then George said "You go ahead, I can't keep up." I felt bad for George, but I knew that if I pushed myself I had a chance of breaking the magical two hour and 30 minute barrier.

I lowered my head into the cold wind and gritted my teeth as I crossed the Rudee Inlet Bridge one last time. Now I only had to make a right turn onto the boardwalk and six more blocks to the finish line, albeit into the wind. When I crossed the finish line I looked up and saw that my time was 2:29:14, good enough for a big personal record and 9th place overall. I fell to the pavement and literally cried for joy because all of my hard work had paid off. I was the top local finisher and beat some very good runners.

The winner of the Shamrock Marathon, Terry Baker, had this to say about the wind to the local newspaper, the Virginian-Pilot. "The wind was ridiculous. As much as it helped us when it was behind us, it hurt us twice as much when we ran into it. I won't say I hit the wall, I hit the wind. The last four-five miles were very, very hard."

I ran several good races in April, 1981. The hard training leading up to March and the fact that I stayed relatively injury free was paying dividends. On April 3, I won the Couples Run 5K on the Virginia Beach boardwalk in 16:10. My wife, Carolyn, ran her 5K in 19:35. We won the title of the fastest couple in Tidewater.

On April 5 I ran the Colonial Relays Half Marathon in Williamsburg, VA. My time of 1:12:36 was 7th overall and 2nd in the 30-39 age division. Next was the Azalea Festival 10K in downtown Norfolk. I ran 33:06 for the 10K and won the 30-34 age division. My final race in April was the Old Hampton Ten Mile. My time was 52:55 for a huge personal record. I have a saying that "If you run a PR then you are on the verge of an injury." I was correct because my right shin was hurting so much that I took six days off leading up the Elizabeth River Run.

In the Elizabeth River Run in Norfolk, VA on May 9 I managed 33:39, which was only good enough for 3rd place in the 30-34 age division. On May 29 I went back to Dr. Young and got an X-ray of the right shin. Fortunately it was not a stress fracture, but I was given Naprosyn and told to rest for a week and to get orthotics for the imbalance in my legs.

On June 13, 1981, I won the 30-34 age division in 16:40 in the St. Judes 5K at Mt. Trashmore in Virginia Beach.

I went back to Charlottesville, VA, for the State AAU Masters Track & Field Championships. I won the 5K in 16:40, got 2nd place in the 10K in 33:48, and 2nd place in the 1500 meter run in 4:25. This was all in one afternoon I might add.

My weekly mileage for July 1981, was 88, 90, 84, 84, and 91. In the middle of these big weeks I ran a 5K in 15:56 and a one mile race in 4:46. From July 26 – August 1, I was a counselor at the Roy Benson Running Camp in Brevard, NC. I got to run with such stars as Mary and Julie Shea, and Randy Thomas from Boston. I ran 91 miles that week in the Blue Ridge Mountains. We ran twice a day and some of the trails were almost straight up. I felt super strong when I returned to flat Norfolk.

On August 8 I was 5th place overall in the Lion's Club 5K in Norfolk in 15:48, which was a new personal record. I was 2nd place overall in the Portsmouth, VA, 5K in 15:58 on August 29.

The Peninsula Track Club's Couples 5K race was held on September 11 at Christopher Newport College. Carolyn and I won the married division by four minutes. My time was 16:19 and Carolyn ran 19:51.

My only other race in September was the Virginia Ten Miler in hilly Lynchburg on September 26th. I ran 56:13 for the ten miles.

On September 28 several members of the Tidewater Striders took turns running from the steps of the Capitol in Washington, D.C. to Virginia Beach, with an American flag given to us by Congressman Bill Whitehurst. This flag was to be flown at the upcoming Neptune Festival in Virginia Beach. We had a police escort and Ronald McDonald in a little motorized car follow us down Route 1 through Fredericksburg and Richmond, then on Route 60 to the Hampton Roads Tunnel.

On October 3 I was 4th place overall in the Mulberry Island Half Marathon at Ft. Eustis, in Newport News, VA. My time was 1:12:42.

The final race for October was the Coliseum Mall 10K in Hampton, VA. This race was advertized as being perfectly flat and capable of a world record, so several world class runners came. They included Rod Dixon from

New Zealand, Benji Durden from Georgia, Jeff Galloway from Georgia, Patti Catalano from Boston, and author George Sheehan from New Jersey. The world record was not broken because there were too many turns on the course. However, they ran some extremely fast times. Dixon's winning time was 28:13 and Patti Catalano ran 34:14. I ran 33:21 and was edged out in the 30-34 age division by Jeff Galloway, who later became famous for his books on running and training method of walking and running to complete a race.

In November of 1981 I set another personal record at the Tidewater Striders 15K in 50:11. On November 15 I won the AAU Virginia State Masters Cross Country Championships in 33:47. I guess I was doing something right because as of November 19 I started getting shoes and clothing from Nike. I would just get a few pair a year, not every month like the World Class runners, but it sure felt good when the UPS truck came with goodies. My last race in November was the annual Turkey Trot in Virginia Beach. I set a PR in 32:35 which was good enough for 5th place overall and first in the 30-34 age division.

On December 5 I placed 3rd overall in the Bethel, NC, Marathon in 2:33:41. Next was the Tidewater Striders 20K run on December 12. I was 5th place overall in 1:10:13.

I closed out 1981 with the Seashore Half Marathon in Virginia Beach on December 26. I ran neck and neck with good friend Pete Gibson and we were both awarded 2nd place in 1:11:32. This was a personal record for me in the half marathon.

85

Chapter 9
The Year of PR's
1982

*"To give anything less than your best
is to sacrifice the gift."*

Steve Prefontaine

My mileage for 1981 was 4,035, or 77 miles a week on the average. I ran some good times and I hoped it could continue. One of my goals was to do well in the Shamrock Marathon on March 20. I continued to stress my body by doing ten or more workouts most weeks. My weekly miles were between 80 and 105 miles per week. I tried to run with someone as much as possible especially on the long runs at Seashore State Park on Sunday mornings. I mostly ran with Greg Eck, Craig Allen, Bill Bernard, Mel Williams, Dave McDonald, Ron Borsheim, and Dan Hurley.

The first race that I ran in 1982 was the Winter Four Miler on January 2 in the Norfolk Botanical Gardens. I ran 20:40 and got 2nd place overall behind future Hall of Famer, Pete Gibson.

I did a killer workout that week of 6 by 1 mile averaging 5:17 with a 440 yard jog in between. I did a total of 16 miles the day before and four miles the morning of this workout then 12 miles the day after. Some of the workouts that we did in those days blow my mind now. One of my favorites came from Coach Chernock at William & Mary.

After a two mile warm up I would do 4 by 880 in 2:30 with a 440 jog in between, then 4 by 440 in 70 seconds with a 220 yard jog, then 4 by 220 in 30 seconds.

Dan Hurley and I often would run "Fartlek" on the Elizabeth River Run course on Hampton Boulevard in Norfolk. We would start at the Armed Forces Staff College and run two minutes hard and a one minute jog for the entire course. Our times of 35-36 minutes would win many races today.

On January 23, I ran the Tidewater Striders 25K and was 7th place overall in 1:28:56 and on February 13 the 30K in 1:45:58. For the rest of February, I concentrated on long runs and piling on the miles to get ready for Shamrock. My weekly mileage for February 1982, was 97, 103, 79, 104, and 104.

I ran two races in March in preparation for the Shamrock Marathon. On March 6 I ran the Walsingham Academy 8-Mile in Williamsburg, VA. My time was 43:43 and I won the 30-34 age division. The following week I drove to Jacksonville, FL with Charlie George for the RRCA National Convention since I was the President of the Tidewater Striders. I ran the Jacksonville River Run 15K in 50:38. It was a flat course, but the 80 degree temperature was difficult to run in.

I thought I was ready for a good time in the Shamrock Marathon on March 20. However, it was an awful day for runners. It was 40 degrees with a 25 mph wind and a hard rain. At 14 miles I had to drop out due to hypothermia. I had never experienced anything like this before. I didn't have much body fat in those days. I was 5'10" tall and weighed 145 pounds or less. I knew something wasn't right after mile ten. My times were slowing down and I wasn't "focused" or able to concentrate. I stopped at a water stop and was so cold they convinced me to stop. I was taken to the tournament hotel by the paramedics and put in a warm tub. It took about five hours for me to stop shivering. Naturally I wasn't wearing many clothes in the race, but I was chilled to the bone. I have always said that I would "rather sweat than shiver." The good thing about dropping out is that, although I wanted to do well in the marathon, I would be still be fresh for races in the near future.

Two days later, the weather improved and I was back to feeling normal, so I resumed training with a vengeance. I decided that I was not going to let that race dampen my spirits, so I entered several races hoping that the hundreds of miles that I put in the tank would pay dividends in the spring races.

On April 17, 1982, I ran the Azalea Festival 10K run in 33 minutes and finished close behind super runner Cletus Griffin. Last year's winner, Dave McDonald decided to run despite arriving six minutes late. McDonald managed to pass all but the first 40 runners, according to race officials, with an estimated time of 33 minutes. Carolyn won the women's open division in 41:04. I was able to beat my training partners Bill Bernard and Dan Hurley and that dynamo Pete Gibson. Sometimes the time that you run in a race isn't as important as who you beat.

Such was the case in the Old Hampton, VA, 10 Miler on April 24. This was a "who's who" of the top local distance runners. It seems that the flat, fast course drew everyone hoping for a fast time. Craig Allen was the winner in 51:54 followed by Rick Thompson in 52:25, Cletus Griffin in 52:43. I was 4th overall and 1st in the 30-34 age division. I was ecstatic with my time of 52:57 especially since it came at the end of a 95 mile week and I beat some top runners including Pete Gibson, John Peele, Steve Frisk, and Bryan Hawley.

I did well in the Elizabeth River Run 10K on May 8 running it in 32:37. However, my time was only good enough for 14th place overall, but I did win the 30-34 age division.

The following Saturday I ran a personal record for the 5K in 15:40 at the Taylor Elementary School Book Run in Norfolk. I had not run a 5K race in several weeks, so I felt ready for a good time.

The race was run on the shaded streets of the West Ghent neighborhood in Norfolk. There were several turns that may have slowed the times a little. My first mile was 4:50 and I hit the two-mile mark in 9:55. I was still with the lead pack and I knew I was on pace for a great time if I could just hold on.

I hit the three-mile mark in 15:10 and the sprint was on! I tried to reach down for that extra gear, but it just wasn't there. I gave it my all, but the top two runners pulled away from me. The winner was Burt Robinson in 15:28, followed by top high school runner James Hammond in 15:31. I felt pretty good about my result, especially when I realize that at 34 years of age I was about twice as old as Hammond.

On May 29 I ran the Yorktown, VA, Victory Run 8 Miler. I was 5th place overall in 43:08, which was a personal record for that distance. I loved this course because it is run on trails connecting the Yorktown battlefield with the town of Yorktown and ends where the surrender by General Cornwallis took place to end the Revolutionary War. Although it was the end of May the trees and paths made it seem much cooler. The winner was top runner Dave McDonald, followed by Virginia Military Institute runner Ed Daniel, and former college runners John Romaine and Craig Allen.

I ran another personal record on June 12 at the Harborfest/Pepsi Challenge 10K in downtown Norfolk. I was very pleased with my time of 32:11 and getting 3rd place. Assistant track coach at Old Dominion University, Dave McDonald, was the overall winner in 30:06 followed by recent high school graduate Ronnie Borsheim in 31:53. Oddly enough, Borsheim was sandwiched between his mentors. He was planning on attending Old Dominion and getting coached by McDonald and I was his high school coach.

On June 19 I ran the St. Judes 5K in the rain and mud around Mt. Trashmore. It was so sloppy that race director, Pete Decker, was instrumental in getting it paved in time for the race in 1983. The city of Virginia Beach has since widened the path around the lake and can easily now accommodate the hundreds of runners in the Turkey Trot 10K on Thanksgiving Day.

On July 3 several of us Tidewater Striders ran the Washington to Belhaven, NC Half Marathon. I was the overall winner in 1:11:41 which was a course record. The highlight of the race for me was riding on a float in their Fourth of July parade. This small town in eastern North Carolina has one of the longest lasting July 4th celebrations in the United States.

I always wanted to do well in the AAU Virginia Masters State Track and Field Championships, so I cut back my training a few days before the races in Charlottesville. I made the three hour drive to Charlottesville the morning of the race to save hotel costs, stopping along the way to stretch. I won the 5K in 16:08 and set a state record in winning the 10K in 33:08. My good friend, Lew Faxon, was entered in the 10K run, but fortunately he had moved up to another age group. We made a pact to run together and take turns sharing the pace and run 80-81 seconds per lap. The 10K is 25 laps around the 440 yard track which can get pretty boring. The plan worked perfectly. As we crossed the start/finish line for another lap the leader would fall back and tuck in behind the other runner to allow him to break the wind and set the pace. I won the 30-39 age division and Faxon won the 40-49 age division. I owe a lot to Lew for pacing me in this race.

I was a counselor again at the Nike Running Camp in Brevard, NC, from July 25-31. I arrived at camp in excellent condition. Anne Audain, from New Zealand was a guest speaker that week, sent by Nike to socialize with the runners. I was extremely appreciative that she allowed me to run with her in many of her training runs. The camp was headquartered at lovely Brevard College with the Pisgah National Forest only a few miles away.

On Monday morning, the first day, Anne and I ran the seven miles up a winding road to determine which group the runners would be in. The fastest to the top were in group one and on down the line. Coach Benson realized a few years later that this was not the best method to put the campers in groups. They were exhausted from this run after the first day.

The next morning, everyone ran seven miles at 6:00 am on the hilly Blue Ridge Parkway. That afternoon, Anne and I ran 20 by 220 yard sprints on a road near the campus with short rest breaks. A few weeks later, she won the Commonwealth Games 3,000 meters in 8:45.5 for a New Zealand and Commonwealth Games record. She had set a world record in the 5K in 15:13 in 1982, so this was no slouch I was running with. In her book, *"Uncommon Heart"* she gave me some of the credit for pushing her in workouts at the running camp. That was very kind of her, but she didn't need my help. I ran 88 miles that week and all of it was on the hills and trails of the Blue Ridge Mountains. My legs were like jelly.

Two days after running camp, I was asked by Dr. Mel Williams to participate in a study in his lab, to determine the effects of bee pollen on endurance. Some of us were given bee pollen capsules and some a placebo for five weeks. We would warm up then start off running on a treadmill at 7:00 per mile on an incline and progressively get faster every minute, as well as increasing the incline. After every minute I was asked how I felt on a scale of one-ten. This was a test of PRE or perceived rate of exhaustion. I was already tired from my week of running camp, but I didn't want to let Dr. Williams think I couldn't stay on that treadmill very long either. I never did find out the results of the test or if bee pollen is helpful or not.

A week after running camp I was exhausted, but stoked to run faster. I ran a 5K in Norfolk on August 7 in 15:59.

On October 2 I ran the Mulberry Island Half-Marathon at Fort Eustis in Newport News, VA. I was in the lead pack the entire race and with two miles to go it was just Rick Thompson and me. We decided not to kill ourselves in a hard run to the finish, but to run together and hold hands at the finish line to signify a tie. We would then flip a coin to determine who would get the first place trophy. When we got to the finish chute, it narrowed down to a single space and I actually have a photo of me crossing the line ahead of Rick. However, at the awards ceremony I was given 2nd place and told that I was beaten by one-tenth of a second. The only thing I can figure is that Rick was running in a Navy jersey on a military base or maybe they thought he was better looking?

The hard runs and high mileage again took its toll on my body. I had a sharp pain in my left foot that wouldn't go away, so I went back to Dr. David Young. He gave me a

Cortisone shot in my heel, which made me scream and black out. I rested for two weeks then ran a 5K in Elizabeth City, NC, on October 31.

On November 14 I ran the Tidewater Striders 15K in 50:56, for 2nd place in the 30-34 age division. My running diary noted that I was now having pains in my right hip, right hamstring, and right lower back. Is this the precursor of what is to come?

In December, I ran a good time of 32:58 at the Coast Guard 10K in Yorktown, VA, and got 4th place overall. It was 78 degrees at the start and very hilly, but I always preferred running in the heat over the cold. The winner was Rick Salazar, the brother of super marathoner Alberto.

In summation, 1982 was a good year. I ran 4,198 miles for an average of 81 per week and set several personal records.

Chapter 10
My Final Marathon
1983

"If I only ran when nothing hurt, I would never run."

Dana Carvey

This was a very difficult and frustrating year. Many of my running injuries started to take their toll. I had surgery for plantar fasciitis in August, and the pain and stiffness in my right hip started to get worse. I was still able to run a few good races, but nothing like in the past.

My first race of 1983 was the Nature Trail Half Marathon in Virginia Beach, on January 1. I ran 1:12:54 and was 3rd place behind future Tidewater Striders Hall of Famer Dave McDonald and Rick Thompson. Then on January 22, I got 2nd place behind future Tidewater Strider Hall of Famer Bill Bernard in the Northwest River 25K in Chesapeake, VA, in 1:27:29.

On February 5 I was the 3rd place overall finisher in the Northwest River 30K in 1:45:27, then ran a 10K in 33:19 on February 19, and got 2nd place in the 35-39 age division. Then I ran the Christopher Newport 10 Mile in 54:26 and won the 35-39 age division.

My goal, as always, was to run a good race in the Shamrock Marathon in March. I was averaging 85 miles a week in ten workouts including five to six miles of sprints. Sunday was a long run of 15-20 miles, usually with good friends Bill Bernard, Greg Eck, or Craig Allen.

March 19 Shamrock day arrived, but so did the heat. Race director Jerry Bocrie said that 1900 runners started the race, but less than 1200 finished. The temperature was 70 degrees at the start and rocketed up to the 80s during the race. My time was 2:33:13, which was good enough for 6th place overall. I was satisfied with the result considering how warm it was and how many runners dropped out. I was beaten by Nick Manchu of Romania, Rick Thompson of Virginia Beach, and by Bill Bernard. The Tidewater Striders Men's Open Team won the 1983 Shamrock Team Championship. The team members included Mike Beckner, Bill Bernard, Randy Cook, Ed Lee, and John Peele.

On March 27 I ran the 5K in 16:06 at the Jewish Community Center in Norfolk. I was 10th place overall, but 1st in the 35-39 age division.

I did a stupid thing on the weekend of April 2 and 3. On April 2 I ran the Franklin, VA, Ten Mile in 55:20 and got 2nd place behind future Tidewater Striders Hall of Famer Pete Gibson. The next morning, I did a ten mile training run at Seashore State Park in Virginia Beach, in 65 minutes, then that afternoon raced a 5K in 16:36. For some reason I thought I was bulletproof or immune to injuries.

On April 10, I ran the Charlottesville, Virginia Ten Mile and won the 35-39 age division. My left foot, heel and arch hurt so much that I took a week off from running. I resumed running on April 18 and ran the Old Hampton Ten Mile on April 23 and won the 35-39 age division.

The pain got worse in my left foot. I would take three to five days off from running, then try to resume training only for it to throb again. It was strange how the pain would vary. When I got up in the morning, it felt like someone was driving a nail through the bottom of my heel. I would start running very slowly and the arch would stretch out after a mile and feel fine. However, by the end of the day, the pain returned. Then it got to the point when it hurt constantly. For the next three months I was only able to run 30-40 miles a week because the left foot hurt so badly. Dr. Young and I decided to have surgery on the foot to repair this tarsal tunnel syndrome. So, I had my first running surgery on August 5, 1983. The stitches were removed on August 15 and I was told to start walking, swimming, or biking.

I said to myself at the time, that I would be satisfied to be a recreational runner content to just run five miles a day at an easy pace when I recovered from this surgery. But, I lied. I could not help myself. The type A personality and competitive urge in me kept telling me that I MUST keep running. As Satchel Paige said, "Don't look back, something might be gaining on you." Of course, he also said, "Avoid running at all costs." I wasn't about to do that. I had too much fun and success when I was healthy to quit running.

I wasn't having much good luck at this time. The first time that I went on a bike ride, I got a flat tire and someone had to come and pick me up. I started running again on September 15. I jogged one mile on the grass, but it felt like a marathon. On September 17 and 18 Greg Eck and I rode our bicycles 100 miles from the other side of the Chesapeake Bay Bridge tunnel to Chincoteague, VA, spent the night, then rode back the next day.

For the rest of 1983, I just tried to baby the foot and come back slowly from the surgery. I had a few good workouts in October, but my foot started to hurt again so I basically backed off for the rest of the year.

Little did I know it at the time, but the Shamrock Marathon in 1983 would be my last marathon. I was looking forward to my birthday in 1983, so I could move into another age division (35-39), but 1983 seemed to be the start of my downfall. I only ran 1876 miles in 1983.

1983 was not only the year of my last marathon, but the year that I got divorced from my wife, Carolyn. We had a beautiful two year old daughter, Jennifer, who has grown up to be a wonderful young lady.

Chapter 11
The Beginning of the End
1984

*"As athletes, we have ups and downs.
Unfortunately you can't pick the days they come on."*

Deena Kastor

My foot was still not 100% in the beginning of 1984, so I embarked on a training regimen of swimming, jogging in the pool, brisk walking, then some light jogging, starting in the middle of January. I wasn't ready to retire from running so I began my comeback!

I ran 42 miles the following week, but the left foot started hurting again so I did not run again until the middle of May. Gee, I wonder if I did too much, too soon?

I started training again on May 19, and immediately ran 49 miles that week to try to make up for lost ground. I was running more often at Seashore State Park for the soft ground and shade. Bill Bernard, Craig Allen, and Greg Eck were my loyal running partners almost every Sunday. In addition, Greg and I did some hard eight to ten mile runs during the week after work. These training runs often turned into races running faster than six minutes per mile on the trails of Seashore or streets of Norfolk.

On August 25 I ran the Portsmouth City Park 5K run in

16:45. It wasn't that fast, but it felt good to be in competition again.

One of the races that I always tried to do well in was the AAU State Masters Track and Field Championships held on the University of Virginia track. So, on September 1 I ran the 10K in the morning in 34:40 for 2nd place in the 30-39 age division then I won the 5K in 16:42 two hours later.

I ran the annual Peninsula Track Club's 5K Couples Run in 16:31 on September 7 and was 2nd place overall. On September 16 I ran another 5K in 16:15. I only ran 50-60 miles a week so I did not expect my times to be as fast as before.

On September 28 I strained my left quadriceps muscle and rested it until October 15. I ran the Elizabeth City, NC, 10K run in 36:03 and was 2nd place overall.

I wanted to run well on November 18 for the Masters National Cross Country Championship 10K in Holmdel, NJ, so I did several speed workouts and raced every weekend to prepare. Lew Faxon, a future Tidewater Strider Hall of Famer, and I, drove to New Jersey in his camper on November 17 for the cross country race. I ran 35 minutes and got 4th place in the 35-39 age division. Faxon got 2nd place in the 45-49 age division.

On November 24 I ran the Crime Line Half Marathon in Norfolk in 1:14:25 and won the 35-39 age group.

I finished 1984 by winning the 35-39 age division in the Road Runners Club of America National 20K

Championship, held at Northwest River Park in Chesapeake, VA, on December 15. My time was 1:11:25 for the 12.4 miles. It wasn't that long before when I could run 13.1 miles faster than that. My times were slower, I could not train as much as I used to, and it seems that I was constantly hurt. I can take solace in the fact that I can call myself a National Champion!

I ran 1,860 miles in 1984, despite missing several days due to injuries.

Chapter 12
Prolonging the Inevitable
1985

"I ran and ran and ran every day,
and I acquired this sense of determination,
this sense of spirit that I would never, never give up,
no matter what else happened."

Wilma Rudolph

I began the year injury free and was averaging 50-70 miles a week. I continued to do long runs of 15 miles or more on Sundays at Seashore State Park with Greg Eck, Bill Bernard, Craig Allen and sometimes others who joined us.

My first race of 1985 was the annual Northwest River Park 25K. I ran 1:33:46 and was 5th overall and won the 35-39 age division. The winner was a former high school runner that I coached, Ronnie Borsheim. He beat his old coach by six minutes, yikes! Lew Faxon was second place in 1:30:31.

In February, I ran the 7th Annual Colonial Half Marathon in Williamsburg, VA. My time of 1:16:08 was only 15th overall, but I won the 35-39 age division. It was 80 degrees at the start, so I was satisfied with my time.

In looking at my training diary I see that I tweaked my right hip and lower back by simply taking out the trash. Little did I know at the time that this could be the start of serious hip problems, which led to a total hip replacement in 1996. A few days later I played two sets of tennis, and then wrote in my log, "STUPID" because it hurt my right hip even more.

On March 2 I ran the Christopher Newport College Ten Mile Run in 56:19 and got 3rd place overall and on March 16, I ran the Shamrock 8K in 26:55. I was not pleased with this race because I was only 6th place in the 35-39 age group.

On March 23 I ran another 5K in 16:30 and got 3rd in the 35-39 age division however; I developed pain in my lower back and inside the left thigh.

I rested my leg, hip, and lower back until June, then I jumped right back into running 50+ miles per week. On June 29 I ran the Amphibious Base 10K in 35:05 and was 5th place overall. Then I developed a viral infection. My primary care physician, Dr. Rudi Schuster, gave me a prescription for Amoxicillin and told me to take a week off.

I ran two races in August 1985. The Portsmouth, VA, City Park 5K in 16:14 and the Couples 5K Run in 16:25. I was feeling better so I upped my weekly mileage to 70-80 miles a week and raced almost weekend.

I see a pattern of stupidity here on my part. Whenever I got an injury, I seldom gave it enough time to heal and when it started to feel better, I jumped back into training and racing full bore. I would say that I deserved what I got, but I wouldn't wish two hip replacements and foot surgery on anyone. It almost seems that I was driven to get trophies or medals, but that wasn't the case at all. Maybe I didn't want certain people to get an award, but I am not sure of that either. In any case I was not a smart runner in retrospect. I wrote earlier how many miles we ran in college and everyone got hurt during their collegiate careers. Then I copy the same training program and wonder why I got injured so often. Shame on me!

When I showed Tommy Neeson one of my training logs where the doctor said to *take a week off from running* and I took one day off and ran ten miles the next day. He burst out laughing saying, "Randy, you might be the biggest idiot I have ever met" or some such kind words. However, I had to agree with him.

In September, I ran the Tidewater 8K in Virginia Beach in 27:36 and won the 35-39 age division, then the Bay Days 10K in Hampton, VA in 33:42 and won my age group again.

On September 28 I ran the very hilly Virginia Ten Miler in Lynchburg in 56:30. Maybe it was because of the hills, but my quads and right lower back cramped near the end of this race.

I ran three races in October: on the 4th it was the Norview High School 5K. I ran 16:29 and got 3rd place overall. On October 12 I ran the Tidewater 8K in Virginia Beach in 27:01 and won the 35-39 age division. I felt stiffness and pain in the right hip joint, so I took some Naprosyn and used a heating pad at night.

On October 16 I went to the free runner's clinic at Old Dominion University and Dr. McCormick said it was "a slight nerve irritation or adductor strain and to take eleven aspirin a day." No, seriously, that's what he said. I actually wrote it down. Maybe he was trying to kill me.

The last race of October was the Norfolk Crime Line Half Marathon on the 26th. I tied for 1st place overall in 1:14:40. I was about a block behind the leader at the half way mark when he accidentally took a wrong turn and cut the course. I yelled to him and the bike leader for him to come back and run the correct route, but he did not. They radioed ahead to the finish line what had happened and since I didn't gain any ground on him after that, they decided to call it a tie.

I foolishly ran five races in November of 1985. On November 2, I ran the Urbanna, VA, Oyster Festival 10K and won the 30-39 age division. The race was run on country roads which were ankle deep with mud the entire race.

On November 17 the Virginia Masters 10K Cross Country Championships was at Mt. Trashmore in Virginia Beach. I ran 34:51 and won the 30-39 State Championship. On November 23 I ran the Northwest River Park 15K Run in 52:21 and got 2nd place in the 35-39 age group.

I formed a Tidewater Striders team and we went to Raleigh, NC on November 28, and won The Athletics Congress Super Nationals Cross Country 5K Classic. The members of this team included Lew Faxon, Greg Eck, Bill

Hart, Roland Parsons, Cletus Griffin and me.

My last race of 1985 was the Nature Trail Half Marathon in Seashore State Park, on December 28. I ran 1:15:41 and was 10th overall and only 4th in the 35-39 age group.

I ran 2,520 miles in 1985 and ran some respectful times and decent races, but I know that I have slowed down and the injuries are adding up.

Chapter 13
All Good Things Must End
1986 - 1987

"Tough times don't last but tough people do."

A.C. Green

I started the New Year off with another injury. This time it was the left knee. Dr. David Young, my orthopedic surgeon, took X-rays which showed inflammation in the knee. He told me to take Naprosyn and not to run for a week.

I heard about a product from Mel Williams called DMSO which is a liniment used on horses. I rubbed this on my knee before running then iced the knee afterwards and it seemed to help some. I was ready for the Kentucky Derby! On January 18, 1986 I ran the Northwest River Park 25K in 1:30:15 and was 4th place overall.

In February, I ran three long distance races and did respectable in all of them. On February 8 it was the Northwest River Park 30K in Chesapeake, VA. My time was 1:49:30 for 4th place overall again and 3rd in my age group. Those 30 year olds were tough. February 16 I ran the Yorktown, VA, 15 Mile Honey Run. It is called this because the winner got a jar of honey. I was the overall winner in 1:29:44. The last race of February was the Colonial Relays Half Marathon in Williamsburg, VA, which I ran in 1:14:58. Surprise, surprise I now had pain in the right knee.

I started coaching my high school tennis team in 1986. They needed a coach and, since I played tennis in high school, I applied and got the position. I needed a break from coaching the track team and the track meets took up every Saturday. I started playing more and more tennis to be able to hit tennis balls with my players and I was playing church league co-ed softball.

In retrospect I would say that mixing these sports with running was not a good thing for my body. We runners are terrible when it comes to giving advice or practicing what we preach.

It is easy to tell someone to rest, relax, and recover from an injury, but there is no way a dedicated runner will follow their own advice. We want to and need to be out there pounding the pavement like mad men to see how much abuse we can dish up to our bodies before crumbling.

In the May 7, 1982 the evening newspaper, *The Ledger-Star,* staff writer Fred Kirsch wrote an article titled "Running Hurt . . . Mega-mile junkies are running hurt (or, quitting is more painful than a shin splint)" If you were to ask most real runners today why they run when they are hurting they will most likely say that it hurts a lot less than not running at all. In most cases, nothing, including throbbing tendons, aching Achilles, sore hamstrings can keep running fanatics from getting their fix of daily running.

In the 1982 Boston Marathon, winner Alberto Salazar staggered to the finish line with a body temperature of 88 degrees. Salazar won the race in an exciting sprint finish with Dick Beardsley then collapsed at the end, winning by two seconds. He was treated in the medical tent and given six liters of water intravenously because he had not drunk during the race. Salazar lost ten pounds of water weight and he only weighed 143.

A runner from Utah was so determined to complete the race that he limped the last 19 miles on a broken leg. When asked why, his answer was "It's just a stress fracture and it's only one broken leg not two and this is the Boston Marathon."

According to Dr. Gabe Mirkin, a physician from Silver Spring, MD, "It's all this competitiveness and big miles. Many people are pushing themselves to their limits. You do that and you're not going to get in shape. You are going to get hurt."

Personally, I had worked so hard over the years to improve and get to my fitness level that the thought of having to stop was too hard to accept. I was paranoid of gaining weight and my competition gaining on me. I knew I didn't have that many more years of quality running left so I kept squeezing everything I had left out of my body.

It's hard to find a serious runner who isn't running with some kind of injury and is still running despite the pain. Local runner Mike McDonald said, "In a way this whole thing has gotten out of hand. When you first start out, all you want to do is get in shape. Then you build up to where all you want to do is finish a marathon. Well, you may run a 3:20 or something. And then you want to run faster than three hours and then its 2:50 so you keep going and going." McDonald added, "I'm great at telling other runners to back off, take aspirin, use ice and see a doctor. Me? I keep putting more and more padding in my shoe and keep on going."

Author Hal Higdon said "Asking a guy who's been out of shape for 20 years and who's discovered the benefits of running to stop because he's hurt is like asking a drunk to walk past a bar. No way."

On August 30 I went to Charlottesville for the State Masters Track and Field Championships. The morning of the race I awoke with a severe pain in the inside of my right thigh. I felt this pain briefly last year, but now it was much worse. I stretched before the first race of the day, the 10K.

In the 10K run I had to run 25 laps around the track or 50 turns and on each turn the pain got worse. Somehow the adrenaline got me through the race and I was able to win the 30-39 age division, but I knew something wasn't right. A few hours later I pushed myself through the State Championships in the 5K to win in 16:45. I later learned that this pain was caused by the hip starting to rotate outward and pulling on the inside of the leg.

I ran two races in September 1986. The first was the Ocean View 5K in Norfolk. I ran 16:28 for the 5K and was 1st place overall. On September 27 I ran the Virginia Ten Miler in Lynchburg in 59:35. It was 80 degrees at the start and extremely hilly especially compared to the flat

Tidewater landscape.

On October 5 I ran the Suffolk, VA, 5K Run in 16:51. I was 6th place overall and 1st in the 35-39 age division.

My training diary for 1986 abruptly ends on October 12 1986. I did a ten mile run at Seashore State Park with Greg Eck and Craig Allen. We ran the ten miles in 62:06 with the first five miles in 33:17 then the last three miles were 5:51, 5:45, and 5:36. I cannot believe that I was able to do this work out because my right hip, lower back, and right inner thigh all hurt so badly. I am sure it was adrenaline and not wanting to let those chumps beat me. I was bent over with pain when I stopped and could barely get in the car to drive home.

I called my orthopedic surgeon, Dr. David Young of the Jordan-Young Institute in Virginia Beach the next day and they were able to squeeze me in that day. I had X-rays taken of the hip joint then spoke to Dr. Young and his Physician's Assistant, Jane Olivo.

When they showed me the X-rays Dr. Young said, "Your running days are over. It's just a matter of time before you will need to have the hip replaced. It all depends on how much pain you can endure. You will know when the time is right, but when the pain affects your lifestyle and your sleep then you will seriously want to consider having the surgery."

I felt like I had been punched in the stomach. I was woozy and my life passed in front of my eyes. After over

20 years of competitive running and logging thousands of miles I was being forced to retire. It was like being told that your best friend had died or just told that your wife wanted a divorce. All I could think was "What will I do, where will I go." All of my friends were runners. Would I see them again? My life, my sleep habits, my weekends were all centered on running.

Needless to say, I was devastated when I left their office. To make matters worse as soon as I got home from Dr. Young's office the UPS truck came to the house with a supply of shoes and clothing from Nike. As a Nike sponsored athlete I would get shoes and clothes a few times a year. I actually sat down and cried when I realized that my running days were over. I had to compose myself and call Nike to tell them that there would be no need to send me any more running gear.

In 1987, I joined the ATC Fitness Center in Norfolk, VA, to try to keep up my cardiovascular fitness level. I went to the gym several days a week and used the stair stepper, rowing machine or elliptical machine up to 60 minutes at a time. I tried to jog some, but the pain was too severe and I was limping more and more. Here I was only 39 years old and had the heart and lungs of a much younger person, but according to Dr. Young, "the bones of an 80 year old."

I have often been asked if it was the running that caused the wear and tear and the arthritis in my joints. I am sure that running up to 5,000 miles a year didn't help, but there is a history of arthritis on my mother's side of the family.

My sister, mother, and grandmother all had severe arthritis. I was told several times that my running form was not ideal because I was an over strider which probably put extra force on my joints.

My right hip joint felt like someone had kicked me with pointed cowboy boots. I limped more and more and was told that I looked like Chester on *Gunsmoke*. I wasn't ready for a total hip replacement at age 39 because I was told that the technology could only guarantee the life of the new joint for ten years. I donated all of my running shoes and clothing to the high school team when Dr. Young told me that I would never run again.

Chapter 14
The First Surgery
1988 – 1996

*"Run when you can, walk when you have to;
crawl if you must, just never give up."*

Dean Karnazes

I started trying to play tennis doubles in 1988, since I could not run. I volunteered at some of the Tidewater Striders races, but it was too depressing to go and not be able to run. I took lessons and went to coaching clinics to be able to help my players. My number one player at Granby High School, Leonard Pabustan, was district champion his sophomore and senior years and played for Old Dominion University when he graduated in 1990.

On August 13, 1992, I made an appointment to see Dr. Young again. His notes state that "Randy Cook is one of my old running partners who I use to run in several marathons with. He has been having some problems with his right hip for a number of years now. Today he states that he has difficulty sleeping on his right side."

After examining me he said that "He has a real bad limp today and carries his right hip with very little motion on walking. He has a circumducted type of gait on the right side. The internal rotation when he flexes his knee up, is about 90 degrees, but when he flexes his knee up or flexes his hip, he does have about a 15 degree external rotation and not able to go to neutral at all. He actually has about a

114

15 degree external rotation flexion contracture."

My X-rays revealed that I had severe osteoarthritic changes of the right hip, with multiple cyst of the acetabulum and loss of almost all of the joint space and sclerosis of the femoral head, as well as that of the acetabulum. In layman's terms this meant that the head of the femur bone was no longer round, it had flattened out so it could not move smoothly and this was obviously causing pain with every step I took.

I returned to Dr. Young on May 20, 1993, for another checkup of the right hip. Dr. Young said that I had a marked limp with osteoarthritic changes of the hip and loss of the joint space. I had a ten degree flexion contracture of the right hip and zero internal rotation. The abduction is only about five degrees and the external rotation is only about ten degrees. We discussed having a total hip replacement but since I was relatively young (45 years old), Dr. Young decided on a conservative approach of Darvocet-N and Naprosyn. I was scheduled for another checkup in six months. If I was doing well, fine, and if not he felt that I should have the total hip replacement surgery within the next year or so depending on how bad the pain is.

I remember that the only way I was able to get any sleep at all during these years, was to drink a couple of beers with my Darvocets and Naprosyns. Yes, I was in a lot of pain but there was never any danger of me getting addicted to these pain killers. I am sure I was not pleasant to be around. It was not an easy thing to be a very competitive runner for over 20 years, then to suddenly have to stop training, stop racing, and no longer be on a daily schedule, and in constant pain to boot, was a lot to try to deal with. Yes, I went to the gym for exercise but, as any runner will attest, nothing beats running for exercise and the pure enjoyment of being outside in the elements with the wind in your hair and the sweat pouring down you or freezing on you in the winter. During my competitive years of running, I completed 15 marathons and hundreds of races and ran thousands of miles in training in all kinds of weather.

The common theme in my career was going from one injury to another. Instead of throwing in the towel and listening to intelligent advice, I simply did what every hard core athlete would do; search for a doctor who said it was okay to keep running. This is what I did until I fell apart. Perhaps in hind sight I should have been a "fitness runner" and just run for exercise or to keep my weight down. However, I was born with a type A personality and have always done everything in my life all out.

On August 17, 1995, I went to see Dr. Young again. I was having a lot of pain and difficulty walking. Dr. Young noticed that I had "An abnormal gait and stiffness of the right hip and is unable to walk with a decent gait. With the loss of range of motion he has to walk with a circumductor type gait at the present time." Also, "He has about five to ten degrees of internal rotation of his right hip and the external rotation is zero. He can only flex to about 90 degrees and abduction is to about five degrees. He has got equal leg lengths at this time."

The X-rays showed that I had severe osteoarthritic changes of the right hip with loss of the joint space with sclerosis of the femur and of the head, as well as the acetabulum and cystic changes of his head as well as that of the acetabulum.

The plan was to "post me" for a total hip replacement sometime in January of 1996. I prolonged the surgery until April 2, 1996, when I was on spring break from teaching then I would be out for the rest of the school year. I checked into Sentara Leigh Hospital in Norfolk, VA, bright and early and had surgery at 7:30 am. I recall that the surgery was on Tuesday morning and they tried to get me up from the bed that evening. When I stood up I blacked out from the pain. I went to physical therapy on Wednesday and Thursday, then I was released on Friday, April 5, 1996.

I was homebound and a prisoner in my own house for six weeks, because I was not allowed to ride in a car for fear that a sudden stop would dislocate the hip. Fortunately the weather was nice and I could sit on the deck and read or else I would have gone crazy.

Physical therapists came to the house two to three times a week to help me exercise the new joint and a nurse came to give me shots of a blood thinner. In the second week, I was rushed to the hospital for X-rays of the lower leg because they were afraid that I had a blood clot. It was a small one so I was not admitted.

I was not a good patient. I wanted to be outside getting exercise and free of pain. At least the pain I was having was from the surgery and would go away soon. I started using a walker, then advanced to crutches after three weeks. I was taught how to go up and down stairs with the crutches, then was allowed to take short walks on my street. A few weeks later, I graduated to a cane and started to feel better about myself. I was released by Dr. Young and physical therapy after six weeks.

I went to my gym, ATC Fitness and climbed on the treadmill to see if I could walk. My goal was to someday be able to walk a mile in 15 minutes. Baby steps, baby steps.

I was still working at the Roy Benson Nike Running Camp in Asheville, NC, in July. Coach Benson graciously found a position for me doing office work and in charge of the "walking wounded." I would walk with the injured, sore, lazy teenage campers and I quickly got to where I could walk three miles on the trails. Instead of a cane I used a "walking stick." I was tired from all of the exercise each day, but it sure felt good to be in the fresh mountain air even if I couldn't run. I appreciate Coach Benson allowing me to hang on as a staff member until 1999.

Chapter 15
The Second Surgery
1997 – 2008

"There's nothing better than adversity.
Every defeat, every heartbreak, every loss contains
its own seed, its own lesson on how to improve."

Og Mandino

I was told that if a patient had one hip replaced, then it is almost certain that they will have to have the other hip replaced. In addition, the technology in 1996 for total hip replacements did not guarantee the life of the replacement much beyond ten years. The artificial socket was fiberglass and the prosthesis was titanium, so there was a good chance that the fiberglass could wear away, meaning a surgery to repair that part of the replacement. Since I was told that my "running days were over," and to avoid any strenuous exercise, I babied the joint. I exercised on the stair stepper or elliptical machine, but not enough to keep from gaining weight. My goal after surgery was to be able to walk one mile in less than 15 minutes pain free.

About four years after the first replacement I started hitting some tennis balls, but did not move very much after a ball. I found someone who was patient with me and hit balls to me, so I did not have to move very much. As I gradually got stronger, I started playing more and more tennis doubles. I enjoyed the exercise, but nothing takes the place of running.

In January 2000 I decided to become a USTA tennis official. I did the class work and took the exams and started to officiate at high school, junior, and USTA adult league events. The problem with tennis officiating is that the tournaments may last 10-12 hours a day and entail a lot of standing and walking. This was not good for my hips or lower back.

Dr. David Young, of the Jordan – Young Institute, retired and his patients were taken over by Dr. James E. Dowd. I met Dr. Dowd on November 16, 2000, when I had an annual follow up visit. Dr. Dowd's notes that day state that "Mr. Cook does fairly well and has occasional achy pain in his right hip, but is otherwise active. He teaches school all day and is actually able to play some doubles tennis. He does have some pain and stiffness in the left hip, which has seen some progression of his arthritis."

The X-rays showed that the left hip has progressed somewhat with about 75% or so joint space loss in the superior acetabulum, with obvious subchrondral sclerosis and osteophytes. Dr. Dowd recommended that I take some glucosamine and chondroitin sulfate pills and the occasional use of antiflammatory medication for the left hip. He would see me again annually or sooner if the left hip got worse.

My next appointment with Dr. Dowd was on August 13, 2001. I told him that I had walked/ jogged the Elizabeth River 10K in May, and was playing tennis almost daily. Dr. Dowd said that my X-rays showed that the left hip has fairly significant degenerative changes, with very narrow joint space and osteophytes present. He cautioned me that running is not a common activity with a hip replacement, so be sensible and not increase my miles or try to improve my times. I listened to his advice and did not run at this time.

I retired from teaching at Norfolk Public Schools at the end of the school year in 2002. I taught in Missouri and Kansas for three years, twenty four years in Norfolk, and used three years of my military service to get full retirement.

On June 17, 2002, my office visit went very well. Dr. Dowd said that I had no symptoms on the right side, but mild discomfort on the left side, however. He encouraged me to keep up my level of activity and we discussed the issues of long term wear.

In 2003, I was seven years out from my first hip replacement surgery. Dr. Dowd discussed that I actually looked quite good and he encouraged me to continue with activities, but not to lose track of following up with annual office visits, given my high level of activity and the growing issues with the left hip.

I was asked by Portsmouth, VA, Public Schools to teach GED classes for adults, 18-years and over, two nights a week. I had to relearn how to do math problems and to teach the students how to write a good essay; the most difficult parts of the course. I take pride in the fact that in the two years that I taught the GED classes, every student who took the exam passed.

In the spring of 2004, I applied for an opening of junior varsity boys and girls tennis coach at Norfolk Collegiate School. I got the position and coached the teams until 2011. Since the majority of the players were beginners and needed to be taught how to play, I did not make cuts. I had as many as 30 players on the team some years. Thanks to the help of parents we were able to do drills with all of the kids and to still be very competitive. In 2006, I was selected as the "Coach of the Year," by USTA Virginia Tennis. I was a very active coach and it took a toll on my hips and lower back. I was also a substitute teacher at Norfolk Collegiate School from 2004-2012.

By 2005, I was having a lot of discomfort in the lower back and left hip. I had a "hunched over" type gait and a slight limp related to the left leg. I also had significant degenerative changes with inner joint space loss and osteophytes present in the left hip. I was given some stretching and extension exercises for the lower back and to help the left hip.

When I saw Dr. Dowd on July 26, 2006, the limp, stiffness in the lower back, and pain in the left hip had all gotten worse. I was now in the "end stage" of arthritis of the left hip with bone-on-bone arthritis and had secondary degenerative changes of the back. We discussed minimally invasive techniques and alternative bearing surfaces. I was to return in a year or sooner if necessary.

In the spring of 2008 we decided to have the hip replaced and set the date for Tuesday, May 27.

I asked Debbie if she would like to walk the Elizabeth River Run 10K on Saturday, May 24 with me. I figured that since I was having surgery in three days what harm would it do to walk six miles. The plan was to start at the very back and just walk casually for the 6.2 miles.

Well, as soon as the race started my competitive juices started flowing and I wanted to walk fast to beat some people ahead of us. Being a self-proclaimed "non-athlete," Debbie had to jog at times to keep up with my fast walking pace. At about the three mile mark, the bottoms of my heels really started to hurt from the way I was walking. I soon realized that I had blood blisters the size of half dollars on both feet. I had to walk on my toes the last two miles.

After the race Debbie said she would never do a "walk" again with a competitive ex-runner. The taste of running was still in my blood.

I checked into the hospital three days later and being prepped for surgery when the nurses saw my feet. One of them yelled at me, "What in the heck did you do to cause these?" When I explained that I walked the 6.2 miles with Debbie she said that "Dr. Dowd may not operate on you when he sees this!"

Dr. Dowd said that if the blisters were closer to another joint, such as the knee, he may not have done the surgery. Fortunately, I was still able to have the left hip replaced at Sentara Leigh Hospital in Norfolk, VA, by Dr. James Dowd and assisted by Physician's Assistant, Ronald Nave. The next day I was out of the bed and went to physical therapy at the hospital. What a humbling experience. I could not move my left leg six inches on its own or without a lot of pain. I suffered through two days of physical therapy at the hospital before being discharged.

The nurses had to treat the blisters and change the bandages on them while I was in the hospital.

When I came home, I had a physical therapist come to my house three days a week for five weeks. I was in extreme pain in both legs, because I had walked bent over for so long and now I was trying to stretch them out. After about three weeks, I progressed to a walker and was allowed to go outside and walk up and down the sidewalk with the therapist. Freedom at last! I gradually increased my distance and got to where I could walk around the block faster and faster.

On June 30, 2008, I returned to Dr. Dowd's office for my first postoperative visit. I was doing better with physical therapy at home, but I still had a lot of pain in the new left hip and had a lot of tenderness in the iliotibial band throughout the lateral thigh. I attribute this to walking with the left leg bent for so many years and trying to straighten it out was causing pain to the point of tears.

To make matters worse, I could not get comfortable to sleep in the bed or even in my favorite recliner. I tossed and turned and writhed in agony. I was given Percocet for the pain and sent to outpatient physical therapy to stretch the hamstring muscles, as well as iliotibial band stretching.

I was released by Dr. Dowd from home confinement after five weeks, which meant that I could also drive if I was careful. I returned to umpiring tennis tournaments in mid July 2008 but I probably should not have. I was on my feet 8-12 hours a day, with very few rest periods at the Girls' 16s National Clay Court Championships in Virginia Beach, VA. I used a cane to walk from court to court. That was either dedication or stupidity.

I went back to Dr. Dowd on July 28 for another follow up visit eight weeks out from the surgery. I had started some light walking and riding my bicycle three-four miles easy in the neighborhood. It was difficult getting on and off the bicycle, so I had to put the bicycle in the street and I stood on the curb and swung my right leg up and around the seat.

The biggest problem I had at this time was swelling in my left ankle, pain in the left hamstring, and numbness in the left foot. I was worried that they had hit a nerve during surgery and I had lost feeling of the foot. Dr. Dowd thought it could be sciatica. I was given a Medrol dose pack to see if that would alleviate the symptoms and some stretching exercises for the hamstrings.

I was told to return to the office on September 11 because I was having so much pain and stiffness in the lower back, numbness in the left foot, and swelling in the left ankle. Dr. Dowd and Ron Nave, the Physician's Assistant, thought the numbness in the foot could be related to something happening in the lower back, or it could be a result of tarsal tunnel surgery on the left foot in 1983. I was

125

sent back to physical therapy for exercises to help with back stability and some stretches for the hamstrings. In addition, I was given another prescription for Medrol Dosepak and one for Naprosyn. I was told that I could exercise if it did not cause any pain.

Chapter 16
Tennis Anyone?

"Tennis has given me this wonderful life and I'm very grateful for it."

Maria Sharapova

When I was told by Dr. Young that my running days were over, as well as playing tennis, I was very distraught. I donated my tennis equipment and most of my running shoes and clothes. In the fall of 1999, Steve Cutchin, the tennis pro at Northside Park in Norfolk, VA, suggested that perhaps I could become a United States Tennis Association official. This would keep me active and it might be something that I would enjoy.

I learned that Old Dominion University was having a home match in January, on campus, so I got there early to talk to the other officials about what steps I would need to take to get certified. I learned that there was going to be a class taught in February 2000, by Jim Bodensick, at Little Creek Amphibious Base in Norfolk. So, I attended the class, joined the USTA, bought a uniform and was ready to start the "shadowing" process. This is when a newbie would work five days, following an experienced official to learn the basics with no pay.

I met Randolph Holland, a fellow high school teacher and coach from Suffolk, VA, in the class and we instantly clicked. He is one of the nicest and best officials I have had the pleasure to work with in my 15 years on court.

On March 27, 2000, I started working and getting paid for my services. In that first year, I officiated several college dual matches, the Atlantic 10 college tournament at Virginia Tech in Blacksburg, VA, three high school tournaments, two small college conference tournaments, and two junior tournaments. I had no issues and got to see some good tennis, but I soon realized that the days could be very long and involved a lot of standing and walking with few if any breaks.

In 2001, I was only able to officiate at two college matches because I had not been trained to be a chair umpire. So, I could only work the lesser matches at first. I still officiated at the Dixie Conference Championships for small colleges, high school district and regional playoffs, the USTA Girls' 16 and under National Clay Court Championships in Virginia Beach, the Junior Olympics National Championships, and USTA Adult league state and regional championships.

I was getting better at officiating and better known and asked to work more often. I realized that I needed to learn how to be a "chair umpire." This would allow me to work at better college matches and to get off my feet. My lower back hurt very much by the end of an eight or ten hour day.

I memorized everything in the rulebook that a chair umpire needed to know and the correct verbiage when calling the score or overruling an incorrect call by a player. Jack Brown, a very experienced official, took the time out of his busy schedule to come to a tournament that I was officiating and sit near me as I sat in the umpire chair for my first match.

So, on January 21, 2002, at Centre Court Racquet Club in Newport News, VA, I was the chair umpire for the finals of the Boys' 16 and under singles. I was extremely nervous sitting in that unfamiliar umpire chair. I worried that I might fall out of the chair or tip it over, call the score incorrectly, mispronounce a player's name, or make an incorrect call. The parents of both players were sitting upstairs in the balcony and could see and hear everything that I did and said. Jack is such an imposing figure that I definitely did not want to embarrass him or have him think that he wasted his time to come and evaluate me. He made me feel great at the end of the match, when he said, "You are already better now than many of our experienced officials."

This was a big step to become a chair umpire. When you are up in that chair, you are a lightning rod and responsible for everything that happens on that court. I learned that I had a talent for being a chair umpire and got asked to work several large events in 2002.

After I officiated several college matches at William and Mary, Old Dominion, and Norfolk State University, I was asked to work at the Colonial Athletic Association Conference Championships in April. In May 2002 I officiated the Division III Women's National Championships at Sweet Briar College in Lynchburg, VA. I also officiated at the Girls' 16s National Clay Court

Championships in Virginia Beach. In addition, I saw plenty of action at high school district, regional, and state championships and USTA Adult League playoffs. In my first year of being a chair umpire, I did a total of 36 matches. Not bad for a rookie.

In 2003, I continued to gain experience doing what I enjoyed the most, being a chair umpire. I was a chair umpire for 44 matches in 2003, mostly at the college level.

By 2004, my reputation as a quality tennis official had spread throughout Virginia and the Mid-Atlantic region. I was asked to be the chair umpire for an exhibition between Fred Stolle and Owen Davidson, against the top two players from Old Dominion University in February. This event was held at Princess Anne Country Club in Virginia Beach, VA. Stolle and Davidson won multiple doubles titles in their younger days at Wimbledon, the French Open, and the Australian Open. When I called the players to the net and was about to do the coin toss, Fred Stolle asked, "Are you going to be calling f...ing foot faults, because that's total BS if you are."

After I caught my breath and kept from gagging I replied "No sir, Mr. Stolle, we are here to play some tennis and give them a show. Just please try not to foot fault too extreme."

The two wily veterans used every trick in the book that they had learned over their many years of experience. The young and talented college players didn't stand a chance against the angles and drop shots employed by Stolle and

Davidson. It still remains as one of the highlights of my fifteen year career.

On March 22 I was asked to work a charity exhibition in Richmond, VA, between Martina Navratilova and Martina Hingis as a linesman. The ladies put on a good show for the spectators drinking their wine and eating their caviar. I was thankful for the opportunity, but I did not think that I would want to actively pursue working the professional circuit.

I did accept another assignment at a professional women's tournament as a lineman in Charlottesville, VA. This was sponsored by Boyd Tinsley, the fiddle player for the Dave Mathews Band, based in Charlottesville. I worked this event for five days and it seemed that I stayed in the bent over position most of the time, watching to see if a tennis ball lands in or out.

Some tennis officials relish these types of tournaments, but in reality, the pay is mediocre and the people in charge are always trying to find fault with some flaw in your technique.

In 2005, I was recognized as the "Tennis Official of the Year," of the Mid-Atlantic region. The Mid Atlantic comprises Virginia, Maryland, Washington, DC, and eastern West Virginia. I was humbled to receive this award in only my 6th year of officiating.

There are two events that highlight 2006 for me. I was asked to be a chair umpire at the NCAA Division III Men's National Tennis Championships held at Fredericksburg,

VA. I was selected to be the chair umpire for the championship singles match. Also in 2006, I was honored as the USTA/Virginia Tennis "Coach of the Year," and my good friend, Randolph Holland, was the "Official of the Year." I was coaching the junior varsity girls' team at Norfolk Collegiate School and I later learned that several of my parents nominated me for this award. I was deeply moved that they felt I did such a good job of instructing their kids.

In 2007, I was the head referee for the NCAA Division III Regionals of the National Tournament in May. Then I was selected to work at the NCAA Division III Women's National Championships in Fredericksburg, VA, and was the chair umpire for the singles and doubles championship matches.

In June, I was chosen to attend the USTA National Chair Academy at Hilton Head, SC, then stay and be a chair umpire for the women's professional tournament. From July 15-22, I officiated at the USTA Girls' 16 and under National Clay Court Championships in Virginia Beach. I was the chair umpire for the singles finals.

The most prestigious event that I worked in 2007, was the Orange Bowl for international players 18 and under at Key Biscayne, FL. This event is held in December, but the "no see-ums" are swarming all over you especially when the sun goes down. Many future college players were in this tournament and it was another great opportunity for me to get exposure to the upper echelon of the USTA as well.

In 2008, I again worked the NCAA Division III Men's and Women's Regionals at the University of Mary Washington. I also worked the Girls' 16s National Clay Court Championships and was the chair umpire for the doubles finals. In addition to several high school tournaments, adult league tournaments, and college dual matches, I was the chair umpire for 67 matches in 2008.

I received excellent evaluations for my work at Key Biscayne and I started to apply for more assignments at the professional level. The USTA started to advertise that the key word was "diversity." They did not admit it to me, but I was 60 years old and not a minority, so basically it would not be worth it to them to train me for the next step at that point in my tennis career. They want young people, females, and other minorities. I understand their stance and I have accepted it.

The pay for such large USTA events as the U.S. Open is paltry compared to our local fees and an official has to work several years before even getting their transportation completely paid for. Except for the top rung of officials at the "Grand Slam" tournaments, most of the linesmen only get $90.00 a day, regardless of how many hours they work. Our local Umpires Association, on the other hand, pays mileage and overtime after eight hours. So, I make more money by staying closer to home, which is fine with me at this point in my life.

Don't get me wrong, I have no problem with traveling and working throughout the Mid-Atlantic region. I make three trips a year to tournaments in Salisbury, MD, and four-five tournaments a year in Fredericksburg, VA; as well as to Richmond, Wintergreen Resort, and Charlottesville.

In 2010, I was selected to work at several prestigious events. In April, I was a linesman at a women's professional tournament in Charlottesville, VA. In May, I was the head referee for the NCAA Division III Women's National Championships at the University of Mary Washington.

I became the head referee for the Girls' 16s National Clay Court Championships in Virginia Beach in 2010, and continue in that capacity today.

On September 22 I was honored by the USTA National headquarters for being one of the few high school coaches across the country who implement a "no-cut" policy for the high school teams. I received a nice framed certificate that said "the USTA offers special thanks to Coach Randy Cook from Norfolk Collegiate School, for the extra efforts that allow young players the opportunity to participate on a team with their friends and represent their school."

In October, I was a linesman again at a women's professional tournament at Kingsmill Resort in Williamsburg, VA. I was pleasantly surprised when I learned that I was voted the Official of the Year, for Virginia. I received a very nice award at a ceremony at the Country Club of Virginia in Richmond on October 23.

In 2011, I was contacted by the office of the Atlantic 10

Conference to be the referee of their tennis championships in the spring. They use two sites, Boar's Head Sports Club in Charlottesville, VA, and the Lindner Tennis Center in Mason, OH. I am the head referee at Boar's Head and the assistant referee in Ohio. Debbie Richardson, Lucas Feller, and all of the other staff members from the A 10 could not be any nicer to work for. We have had a fantastic working agreement since 2011, and I hope it continues.

I officiated 25-30 college dual matches in 2011, in addition to multiple USTA tournaments, and I was the chair umpire for 59 individual matches.

In 2011, I was appointed by USTA Virginia Tennis to be the Chairman of Tennis Officials for 2011 and 2012. In this prestigious position I helped recruit and train new officials, and make sure that all tennis tournaments were staffed with qualified officials.

The highlight of 2012 was being selected to officiate at the Boys 18 and Under National Hard Court Championships in Kalamazoo, MI. Well, it was mostly a good experience. Upon arriving I learned that I had a roommate from Florida named Chris. When he checked into the room, he immediately emptied his suitcase on the floor. He laid on the bed to take and nap and when he woke up, he saw a little black bug, but didn't think anything of it. Two days later his upper body looked like he had been stung by a thousand wasps. Chris asked if I knew what it could be, but I had no idea. He said, "I'm going to show the manager and see what they say."

Well, within five minutes, the desk clerk and three maintenance workers were in our room looking for bed bugs. Sure enough, they found bed bugs in Chris's bed, but not mine. I think Chris might have brought them with him in his clothes that he dumped on the floor. Regardless, they moved us to another room and we had to stay up all night washing our clothes, then running them through the dryer twice, to make sure we killed the bugs. Needless to say, I was exhausted the next few days until I caught up on my sleep. Chris and I were the butt of many jokes for the rest of the tournament.

I did not apply to work at Kalamazoo in 2013, to give the hotel a chance to get rid of the bugs.

In 2013, I promised my wife that I would cut back on working so many tennis tournaments unless she could travel with me. We make three trips to Salisbury, MD, and stay with tournament official, Randy Halfpap, and his lovely family. The rest of 2013, I mainly worked in the local area.

Chapter 17
My Hard Work is Rewarded

2009 – 2011

"This is not about instant gratification.
You have to work hard for it, sweat for it,
giving up sleeping in on Sunday morning."

Lauren Fessenden

In April of 2009 I met David Kidd, a teacher and tennis coach at Norfolk Academy. In the USTA "Find a Partner Program," a member submits their address and skill level on the website and how far they are willing to travel to find a tennis partner. David and I met at the Larchmont public courts in Norfolk and instantly clicked, because we loved to do tennis drills and just hit tennis balls for fitness. David gradually moved me from corner to corner, as I got stronger and we would see how many ground strokes we could hit in a row before someone missed.

On May 21, 2009, I returned to Dr. Dowd's office for my annual follow up visit. At this time I was doing much, much better. Yes, I got occasional aches and pains, but my range of motion was pain free and the numbness was gone in the left foot. I was told that I could continue to exercise "as tolerated."

David and I decided to enter the prestigious Banana Open Doubles Tournament at the Virginia Beach Tennis and Country Club in August 2009. I was lucky to have found David as my tennis partner because he is much younger and an excellent player. With his powerful serve and net play, and my endurance and steady ground strokes, we reached the finals, but lost to a team from Kentucky in a third set tiebreaker. We qualified for the National Championships in Hilton Head, SC, but were unable to go because of previous commitments.

I continued to practice and do tennis drills as long as the weather permitted through 2010, with David. I could feel myself getting stronger and in better shape as I worked out on the elliptical machine at the Norfolk Wellness Center three-four times a week, up to 60 minutes at a time, rode my stationary bicycle, and started walking in the neighborhood.

On May 12, 2010, I was examined for my annual follow up visit by Ron Nave. I let him know that I was fairly active on the elliptical machine, playing tennis, and on my feet several hours at a time, when I umpire tennis tournaments. I continued to have stiffness in the lower back. I was given another prescription for Medrol-Dosepak and some exercises for the lower back.

David and I entered the Banana Open Tournament again in August 2010. We lost in the finals again in 2010: 7-6, 6-4 to two 30 year olds. David and I again qualified for the Banana Open National Championships in Hilton Head, SC, but opted not to go.

In November 2010 I was recognized as the USTA Virginia Tennis "Official of the Year," and I was appointed the Chairman of Officials for Virginia tennis officials for 2011 and 2012.

On February 26, 2011, I was inducted into the Tidewater Striders Running Club Hall of Fame. Below is a summary of my achievements that appeared in the program the night of the ceremony at Ft. Story Officers Club in Virginia Beach, VA.

- Charter Member of the Tidewater Striders
- Tidewater Striders Vice President (1981) and president (1982)
- National Champion in the 20K for 35-39 age group (1984)
- Previous state record holder for Submaster (30-39) 10K on the track
- Virginia State Champion as a submaster (30-39) and master (40-49)
    - Cross country (4 times)
    - 5K on the track (4 times)
    - 10K on the track (6 times)
- Top 10 finisher overall in the 1981 and 1983 Shamrock marathon
- 4th place overall in the United States for the one hour run on the track (1978)
- Named "Most Outstanding Submaster" (30-39 age group) at the Virginia State Masters Track Championships (1982)
- Personal bests: 5K, 15:40; 10K, 32:11; 10 miles, 52:55; 1/2 marathon, 1:11:32; marathon, 2:29:14
- Tidewater Striders Grand Prix award winner for multiple years

Being elected into the inaugural class (2011) of the

Tidewater Striders Hall of Fame was an incredible honor. There were ten people inducted that night and I was in awe to be in such company. The other members of the class of 2011 are: Jerry Bocrie, Rick and Sharon Brown, Cokey Daman, Dan Edwards, Charlie George, Dave McDonald, Bee McLeod, Raymond Ochs and Mel Williams.

I remember Dave McDonald when he ran the 1980 Shamrock Marathon and finished in a three way tie for first place. The following year I was driving down Hampton Boulevard in Norfolk, VA when I spotted someone who resembled McDonald. I pulled the car over and said, "Aren't you Dave McDonald the runner?" He replied that he was and that he had just moved to Norfolk to get another degree at Old Dominion University.

We became good friends and ran several training runs together when he had an easy day so I could keep up. His marathon pr and mine are almost ten minutes apart so I had to work hard to keep up with him on our runs. Dave is one of the nicest guys around and was one of the fastest runners in the area for several years.

I have known Mel Williams longer than anyone in the Tidewater Striders. We first met in the mid 1970s when I came home from college on vacation. "The Professor," as most people call him, is the epitome of a Southern gentleman even if he is from the north. Mel has served on the Board of Directors for more years than anyone, served on committees, written dozens of books and is always there to assist a struggling writer or a new runner. In my mind Mel is Mr. Tidewater Strider. To date, Mel has run all 35 of the Marine Corps Marathons, one of four men to have done so.

On June 2, 2011, I was seen by Ron Nave for my annual follow up visit. It was noted that both hips moved well and I did not have any pain with straight leg raises. However, X-rays showed that the right hip joint, which was replaced in 1996, was showing wear in the fiberglass socket. We discussed that if this wear pattern continued, I would have to have the socket replaced.

Chapter 18

The Comeback Kid

2012- 2013

"You can't go back and make a brand new start, but you can start now and make a brand new end."

Jack Garmise

I started running/jogging again on March 2, 2012. There was not one specific reason why I put on the running shoes again, but several things that gave me the urge to get back out there. First, I had gained some weight in the 25 years of not running and didn't like the way I looked in the mirror. Secondly, my step daughter, Brittany Gleason, had taken up running and I wanted to be able to jog a few miles with her when she came home from graduate school at the University of Texas. Another reason is that after I was elected to the Tidewater Striders Hall of Fame in 2011, I was inspired to want to be part of the running scene again. Now I had to see if it could be done, that is, running after two hip replacements. I have read about other runners doing this, but they were not my age and did not go 25 years in between running.

I discussed the possibility of running with Dr. Dowd and Physician's Assistant, Ron Nave, and they said that if I promised to take it easy and not to do too many miles, or try to run too fast, then it would be okay.

I knew that I would need to be brought up to date on the

latest running shoes, so I went to see Mike Robinson, the owner of Running Etc. in Norfolk, VA. Mike asked how much I planned to run and on what surfaces and made some recommendations. Since I have always been partial to Nike, I decided on the Pegasus 28s. They have been around so long that the Pegasus is given a number for each version of the shoe. I can remember wearing the original Nike Pegasus.

My first goal was to see if I could just complete one mile without stopping. I was able to complete the run; however, to say that I was sore the next day was an understatement. Once I got past the half way point and realized that I could make it home without stopping, I must have been grinning from ear to ear. As I have often said, nothing beats running for exercise and the thrill that one gets from seeing different scenery, plus the satisfaction of sweating and huffing and puffing and getting in better shape.

In that first week, I ran a grand total of five miles, but the pace was slower than 11 minutes per mile. There was a time when I thought it was impossible to run slower than a seven minute mile, but at this point in my life, with all that I have endured, I was satisfied with anything faster than a fast walking pace. In addition to running again, I was riding the exercise bicycle and doing the elliptical machine between 30-60 minutes, at least twice a week, to help with my strength and endurance.

The most important thing about this first week of running is that my hip joints did not bother me. My legs were sore from using different muscles, but it seemed that if I took it easy I might be able to run again.

In my second week of running, I ran four times for a total of nine miles. On Saturday, March 10, 2012, I got bold and thought I would see if I could run three miles nonstop. I used the Garmin Forerunner 10 that my wife, Debbie, gave me to map out a three mile course. I figured that if I ran slow enough I could complete the run. I did my first three mile run in 25 years in 33 minutes, but now I had a measuring stick to compare future runs against.

At the end of March, I sent an email to the residents of my Colonial Place neighborhood in Norfolk, to see if anyone would like to meet for runs two-three times a week. I was able to recruit four runners and we ran between three-four miles. We called ourselves the Colonial Place Pacers. The members were Randy Cook, Sandy Dicarlo, Lee Lamonica, Beverly Vincent, and Cheryl Wagner.

My mileage for March and April of 2012 hovered around ten miles per week, partly because I did not want to push it and also because of my busy tennis umpiring schedule. Some days I was working ten hours or more and didn't have the time or energy to try to run. On May 1, 2012, I did my longest run of four miles in 41 minutes. I then set a goal to run the Elizabeth River 10K on May 26 nonstop and at 10:00 per mile pace.

On May 13 while in Fredericksburg, VA, for the NCAA tennis tournament, I did a five mile run around the Civil War battlefield. I wasn't concerned about the pace at the time, but I was just elated to be able to run this far. My confidence was growing that I could complete the 10K in two weeks. My mileage for this week was 15 miles. I recall the days when I would do that in one day, but baby steps, baby steps.

My annual follow up visit with Dr. Dowd was on May 24, 2012. I told him that I was doing some light running in addition to the elliptical machine. I admitted that I was planning on running a 10K (6.2 miles) in three days. He wished me luck and told me not to push it. My thoughts were "Hip! Hip! Hooray! I'm running again!" My X-rays did not show any additional wear in the right hip socket, which was encouraging to say the least.

The day of my first race in 25 years had arrived, May 27, 2012. I was extremely nervous as I lined up for the Elizabeth River Run 10K in Portsmouth, VA. The temperature was in the 70s at the start, with typical high humidity for southeast Virginia in late spring. The plan was to go out conservatively, run my own race and just try to complete the course nonstop. My "split times" for each mile were 10:05, 19:46, 29:35, 39:47, 49:52, and 60:05 for six miles and 62:18 for the 10K. I slowed down the second half of the race, partly because I started out too fast, the high temperature, and I had not been running enough. I now realized two things, I would need to run more miles and more often if I hoped to bring my times down and I probably should not be running anything longer than a 10K. The competitive juices were flowing again, so instead of just being content with finishing a race, I wanted to compete for an award and try to run faster and faster.

It felt incredible to be out there participating in races again after a twenty five year hiatus. Yes, I had obviously slowed down considerably and had gained forty pounds. However, it was such a thrill to pin that race number on and to hear the starter's gun go off again.

I could not wait until the next opportunity to lace up the racing shoes and put on my racing singlet given me by Running Etc.

For the next five weeks I was averaging 15 miles per week. My next race was the Independence Day 5K in Virginia Beach, VA, on July 4. My goal was to try to run faster than 10:00 per mile pace. My mile times were 9:35, 19:07 at the two mile mark, 28:50 at the three mile and 29:45 for the 5K. I was satisfied with my effort since it was 81 degrees at the start.

My running partner, Lee Lamonica, was preparing for the Crawlin' Crab Half Marathon in Hampton, VA, in October, so we decided to run eight miles on July 29. My wife, Debbie, met us along the loop with water, so we were able to make it without stopping.

Debbie and I met online and had our first date on March 25, 2007. The first time that she invited me to dinner she wowed me with her lasagna and Greek salad and I thought "Wow, I want to see more of this good looking blonde." We started to see more and more of each other and I soon fell in love with her. I proposed to Debbie on October 18,

2008 which was also her birthday. I arranged a surprise birthday party for her. Her daughters Lindsey and Brittany were both there. Brittany flew in from Austin, TX just for the party. When everyone arrived, Debbie and I broke the news of the engagement. We were married on May 23, 2009. My daughter Jennifer and Lindsey and Brittany were all part of the wedding ceremony.

For the month of September 2012 I was up to running 15-20 miles per week and still running with Lee Lamonica, Cheryl Wagner, and Sandy Dicarlo, at least twice a week. These "Colonial Place Pacers" had no idea how much I needed them for motivation and to help get me through each run.

My favorite running store, Running Etc., allowed me to be a member of their Ambassador Program. They outfitted me in a uniform and gave me good discounts on shoes and I would display the store name when I ran. The guys at the Norfolk store, owner Mike Robinson, John Lamogda, Drew Midland, Doug Dugroo and Shannon Ralston, are extremely knowledgeable about running and have supported my comeback.

I ran the most miles in one week in many years from October 8-14. Debbie and I left on October 14 for a six day cruise to the Bahamas. We landed in Nassau on Tuesday, October 16, and while Debbie was shopping, I ran four miles with a coaching friend from Nassau, Steven Murray. It was 86 degrees when we ran at noon and I was suffering, but Steven was kind enough to slow down for me.

I wanted to run with Steven again before the ship cast off and the only time to do it was at 5:00 am. Steven met me outside the terminal and we ran three miles from the ship to the Atlantis resort and back over the Sidney Poitier Bridge.

Steven is one of the track and field coaches for the Bahamas National Track Team. We first met when he brought a group of young kids to the Nike Running Camp in Asheville, NC, in 1990. He was trying to make them stronger for their sprint races by running on the mountainous trails. Since there is nothing in Nassau higher than the one bridge, these kids struggled when they ran everyday, but enjoyed every mile that they ran. After the first few days, several of the younger kids were walking as much as they were running, because they were so sore. However, the "Nassau" kids were the hit of the running camp because they were always smiling and enjoying life.

Debbie and I were dumbfounded when Steven gave us shirts and jackets from the Bahamas Olympic Team. When our ship landed at Freeport the next day, I ran three miles in one of the new shirts that Steven gave me, while Debbie was shopping. I turned a lot of heads and had people wondering how I got that shirt.

In November, my old tennis partner, David Kidd, decided that he needed a break from tennis and started running with me on weekends. Being twenty years younger than me, David quickly got in shape and had no trouble keeping up with the old man.

I ran my first 5K in the comeback on November 12, in Chesapeake, VA, at the Run for Music 5K. I didn't know until I arrived that it was on a hilly cross country course, so I wasn't too disappointed with my time of 31:40, especially since I ran five miles the day before. I got 2nd place in the 55 and over age group, my first medal in "the comeback."

On Thanksgiving Day of 2012, I ran the Tidewater Striders Turkey Trot 10K. My mile times were 9:41, 19:05, 28:37, 38:20, 48:20, and 58:20 and the 10K time was 60:29. This was a post surgery personal record for the 10K! I had pushed myself for my current condition and boy, did I feel it the next two days. My quads were especially sore.

I did several four-five mile runs in the next two weeks, to recover from the Turkey Trot, and to try to build up my base mileage.

My next race was the Santa Shuffle 5K in Portsmouth, VA, and I was hoping for a good time. I ran 28:19 and my mile times were 9:05, 18:10, 27:24 and 28:19 for the 5K distance. It was only good enough for 8th place in the 60 & over age division however.

In 2012, I ran a grand total of 658 miles, but that was in slightly less than ten months.

I started 2013 with two issues that will continue to haunt me all year. First, was an inguinal hernia that had been bothering me off and on for several years. It had gotten to the point where it hurt and burned just from standing a few hours while umpiring. It usually didn't bother me during a run and it went away at night when I laid down. Secondly, my left calf muscle and left hamstring were hurting me and forcing me to miss days of running.

On January 30, my birthday, I ran eight miles. It would be a way to celebrate if I could complete the run nonstop. My time at the 10K mark was 60:42, or 9:46 per mile pace. I felt like I was getting stronger and faster! I did my first speed workout in many, many years on February 5. After a one mile jog, I did three miles of Fartlek where I would run a minute hard, then a minute jog, two minutes hard and a two minute jog, then three minutes hard and a three minute jog. I continued this pattern for three miles. I ended the workout with a one mile jog. It felt just like the old days of competition except half as fast.

I ran the Falcon 5K on March 9 at Cox High School in Virginia Beach, VA. My time for the race was 28:10 and I was 3rd place in the 60 and over category. The mile times were 8:54, 9:10, and 8:57. This was another post surgery personal record.

On March 1 I ran on the trails of First Landing State Park in Virginia Beach, for the first time since 1986. I ran with John McGovern, my wife's brother in law and owner of Ocean Creek Apparel in Virginia Beach. John was kind enough to run slow enough for me to hang on and run 11 miles with him. I hurt from the waist down, but especially in the lower back. I am sure that my posture is very poor from the hip surgeries and walking stooped over for so long. Also, my running gait has changed dramatically and I cannot take the long strides like I used to, because it would put too much pressure on the hip joints.

I obviously overdid it on that run because two days later, while trying to do a speed workout, my entire back seized up on me. I was able to limp home, but was in so much pain that I could not sleep. I went to Dr. Whitehurst, my family doctor, and was given some muscle relaxers. I was really bummed because it bothered me for days to come and when we went to Austin, TX, on March 30, to see Brittany, my stepdaughter, I could barely jog with her. I used ice, heat, and pain pills just to be able to jog an easy three-four miles.

My next race in 2013 was on April 13. It was the Old Dominion University Cub Run 5K in Norfolk, VA. I ran the course in 27:26 which was another post surgery personal best time, plus I got 2nd place in the 50 & over age division. It isn't easy competing against someone in their 50s when I am 65 years old.

For the next six weeks I went to physical therapy twice a week for my lower back and hip flexor muscles at In Motion Physical Therapy in Norfolk, VA. I have never been treated with such patience, kindness, and professional care. The physical therapists who helped me were Alex and Carrie, and they could not understand how or why a 65 year old man with two hip replacements expected to run, let alone try to compete in races. Why does anyone climb a mountain - because it's there. They frowned at me when I told them about my workouts and weekly mileage. In spite of the off and on stiffness in the back and hips, I was consistently running 25-30 miles per week in five runs a week and my runs were getting faster and felt easier.

By the end of April 2013 the Colonial Place Pacers had all but dissolved. Cheryl moved away, Sandy was injured, and Lee and Beverly could no longer commit to a regular schedule.

My last visit to Dr. Dowd was on May 20, 2013. I let him know that I was running 25 miles per week. Also, since I had stopped playing tennis and was now running, my hips were not bothering me as much. However, my lower back continued to bother me. The pain and stiffness moves around and some days are worse than others. I strongly believe that the back, hamstring, and calf issues all go back to my high mileage in the 70s and 80s, leaning forward while running, and subsequent poor posture.

I reconnected with old friend and runner, Ed Lee, and we began running five miles very hard on Wednesday mornings. Ed is younger and faster and pushed me in these runs. I began running the workouts almost as fast as race pace and felt ready to run a good time in the Elizabeth River Run 10K on May 25.

I will be forever grateful to Ed Lee for agreeing to pace me in the race. It was a very cold and windy day for the end of May, and we would have the wind in our faces and beside us for the first four miles. The plan was to start out conservatively, so that I would have something left for the last two miles with the wind at my back.

The majority of the course was along the seawall of the

Elizabeth River in Portsmouth, VA. It was so windy that there were white caps on the water. When the race started, I tucked in behind Ed and just hung on for dear life for as long as I could. If I started to lag behind, Ed would slow down a little and I would surge to catch back up. We crossed the finish line in 56:00 and I was 3rd place in the 65 & over age division. This was the Road Runners Club of America Virginia 10K State Championship, so I beat some good runners in my age group. I was very happy and proud of my race result and it was the fastest 10K since my surgeries.

For the next two weeks, I did several runs between five-seven miles and a ten mile run at First Landing State Park, averaging 9:36 per mile on June 15.

I ran another personal record at the Independence Day 5K at the Virginia Beach YMCA. My time of 27:25 was 2nd place in the 65-69 age group. It was 80 degrees and very humid when the race started at 8:00 am and the first mile was 8:29, but I didn't slow down too much.

The next Tidewater Striders race was the Striders Mile on August 17 at Tallwood High School in Virginia Beach. I ran the one mile in 8:15.2 and got 2nd place in the 65-69 age group.

The Tidewater Striders had an auction for entries to the Rock 'N Roll Half Marathon in Virginia Beach, on September 1. I won one of entries to the race; however, I did not receive notification until a week before the race. By this time it was too late to do a long run and adequately prepare to run 13.1 miles especially in the heat. I tried very hard to run smart by starting off slowly. My only goal was to complete the race without stopping. My goal pace was 10:00 – 10:15 per mile pace. The crowd, the atmosphere, and adrenaline got the best of me and I started too fast. The first mile was 9:40, but it felt easy. I felt great until eight miles and was still under 10:00 mile pace. Then suddenly the sun popped out and the heat, humidity, and lack of preparation got to me. I completed the race without stopping, but the last three miles was agony. I was totally depleted of fluids, despite drinking water at every aid station. I was never so glad to see the finish line of a race and to have Debbie waiting there for me. She helped get me to the aid station where they got some fluids in me and my body temperature down. I was embarrassed that I was being attended to at an aid station, but it was a good thing that I went. I was already stiff and sore in every muscle from the lower back down. This had to be one of the dumbest things I ever did. No one can expect to run a distance race without preparing for it, especially if you have had hips replaced and I should have known better.

After I ran the Rock n Roll Half Marathon, my body was beat up. My lower back and quads hurt and I never knew how or if I would be able to run the next day, until I stretched then took the first steps. Some days there would be no pain and I could "fly," other days there would be pain or stiffness the entire run. I would use ice, foam roller, rolling stick, massage, and heating pad to try to heal and get ready for the next run.

On October 9 near the end of an easy four mile run, my left calf and foot got tight and numb. Debbie and I left Norfolk on October 13 for a cruise to the Bahamas, and I desperately wanted to run with my friend Steven, plus I planned to run a 5K in Norfolk when I returned. I ran three miles with Steven two days later, but had to cut the run short because of the pain. I had difficulty sleeping on the cruise ship because of the pain, which had spread to the lower back, left hamstring, and both hips.

I decided to run the From Here to Eternity 5K on October 19 since I had already entered. I basically had to limp through the race. My time of 29:30 did place me 2nd in the 60 & over age division. Was a medal worth aggravating the injury? Probably not. I rested the body most of the next week and ran the Spooktacular 5K in Windsor, NC, on the 26, because we had already booked a stay at a bed and breakfast. Debbie was going to run her first one mile race, so I decided to run with her. I ran faster than the previous week in 28:36 and got 3rd place in the 60 & over category.

For the next several weeks, I babied the left hamstring, which was now the main culprit. I jogged with Debbie from two-three miles a few times a week. We entered the Jingle Bell 5K run for Arthritis on November 23 in Norfolk. I ran with Debbie, as she ran her first 5K race. Her time was 40:08 and she was 3rd place in her age division!

I am extremely proud of my wife. In the fall of 2013, her health insurance provider required her to have a health coach. This "coach" would call once a month to see if Debbie was exercising and giving her healthy eating tips.

So, Debbie decided to start walking one mile on the weekends. I convinced her that she could jog a mile nonstop if she paced herself. In October 2013 Debbie ran her first nonstop mile and was hooked on running and exercise. She went from one mile nonstop, to three miles in two weeks.

If her work schedule allowed more time to run, she would drop her time by huge chunks. She now runs four miles a day on the weekends and no longer has to have a health coach. She is even more beautiful now than the day I met her!

I started hurting in all parts of the lower back, left hamstring, right hip and right gluteus muscle, and felt twinges in the left hamstring, if I ran much faster than a jog. In addition, the inguinal hernia of my left side was throbbing and burning from standing short periods of time.

On December 28 I met Tommy Neeson from Virginia Beach, the author of *Four Million Steps, From Maine to Florida...and all the Memories in Between.* Tommy is a running addict and more than one person has called him crazy.

He set a world record in 2007 running 50 kilometers on a treadmill to help raise money for the Norfolk Ronald McDonald House. In the book above, Tommy described how he ran from Bangor, ME to Jacksonville, FL in 2008 without any crew or van support. He averaged running over 30 miles a day pushing a baby stroller filled with 60 pounds of clothes, food, water and other supplies to honor his daughter Randi who passed away.

You won't find a nicer and crazier guy than Tommy Neeson. He might even give you the shirt off his back. I keep hinting that I want a certain shirt of his, but he won't give it up.

The first time we met we ran five miles together at First Landing State Park. After introductions we started running and talking, or rather Tommy started talking. I think I was able to get in five words in five miles.

He could have run much faster, but kept the pace slow enough that I could keep up. It seemed that every runner we passed either knew Tommy, or knew of Tommy. I was wondering why they all seemed to go to the other side of the trail to avoid him. I thought I might be ostracized for running with this guy, but I immediately took a liking to him. I was so touched by reading his book that I became motivated to put my story in words. I ran the idea by Tommy and without any hesitation he jumped at the chance to help me in any way possible.

I ran 978 miles in 2013, for an average of only 18 miles per week. There were far too many injuries, but I did run some good races.

I had several good four-five mile runs in early January of 2014, but the pain in the left calf would not go away and the hernia got worse. After talking to Dr. Charles Ives, we decided to schedule surgery to repair the hernia on January 22. I hoped that all of my nagging injuries would heal while

I recovered from the surgery.

Dr. Ives released me on February 27 to start running and exercising again and I did a four mile run, at ten minute mile pace, immediately after the appointment. Even though I missed six weeks of running while recovering from this latest surgery, it seemed like an eternity. I have come too far after twenty five years of non-running to give up now.

What are my plans or goals for the future? To run as much and as often as possible, while enjoying every mile while doing it.

I recognize the fact that I have this opportunity to run again, but for how long, no one knows. Now that I am 66 years old I am at the twilight of my career. I hope to still be able to run when I am 76 or 86 but will the hip joints hold up that long? Only time will tell, but I always believed that it is better to wear out than to rust out.

I promised my doctors and my body that I will run in moderation and not worry about trying to win my age group if I enter a race. I am mixing in cross training at the gym on the elliptical machine and stretching after my runs to try to avoid any injuries. I have come to the realization that it is better to run slowly and enjoy it than to run too fast, get injured and not be able to run at all. If I had another setback now after all that I have been through, I would be devastated.

My motto is "a good day is when I get to run, a great day is when I inspire someone else to run." I just hope that when someone sees me out on the roads plugging away regardless of the weather they might consider taking up jogging or going for a run that day if they were thinking of being lazy. Hey, if I can do it then you can do it! I know that I have inspired my wife to start jogging and it is rewarding to see her enjoy it so much.

Chapter 19
Conclusion

"You don't stop running because you get old;
you get old because you stop running"

Christopher McDougall

Looking back over my running career, I often wonder why I continued to run. I had injuries and surgeries to every part of my body from the waist down. My running logs have many days where an injury is mentioned to heels, knees, hamstrings, thighs, lower back, hips, calf muscles, sore ankles, and plantar fasciitis. I had surgery on my left foot for plantar fasciitis, cortisone shots in my heel and knees, and had both hips replaced.

I spent time in the doctor's office and missed workouts due to pneumonia, sore throats, bad colds, the flu, and every other illness that happened to be going around at the time.

I ran in the Kansas winters when it was snowing and zero degrees, and the summers of Virginia and Kansas when it was 100 degrees. I ran countless hill repeats, mile repeats, and sprints on the track, Fartlek runs, and thousands of miles of distance training.

I was disappointed that my parents were never able to come to a race or see me compete during my competitive years. My father worked long hours and my mother did not know how to drive. Hopefully, I made them proud.

My mother used to say when I got arthritis in my hips that it was caused "by running around town in that damn cold weather in nothing but your underwear," as she referred to my short running shorts of the day. If she had her way, I would have played tennis at Wimbledon, but that was out of the question.

This quote by Steve Prefontaine sums up my feelings. "You have to wonder at times what you're doing out there. Over the years, I've given myself a thousand reasons to keep running, but it always comes back to where it started. It comes down to self satisfaction and a sense of achievement."

Anne Audain, former world record holder in the 5,000 meters, once told me that to be a good runner, one must be confident, be committed, be consistent, and be coachable. I have tried to be all of those things during my running career.

I hope that by reading this book you have learned more of what kind of a runner and person you are. If I have inspired at least one runner to run longer, faster, or for someone to begin a running program then I will be happy.

ACKNOWLEDGEMENTS

Tommy Neeson, I was inspired by your book and your story. Thank you for your encouragement, support and guidance with writing this book. Hopefully we can inspire others.

Co-editor: Terry Lederer. Thanks for teaching me about grammar and commas.

The following people have been instrumental in my life and especially in my running career:

Coach Scrap Chandler, Coach Lou Plummer at Old Dominion University, and teammates Wayne Buyalos, Pete Egan, Doug Mallory.

My coach and teammates at Pittsburg State University: Coach David Suenram, Coach Russ Jewett, Mike Nixon, Wally Autem, Larry Grecian, Marcus Canipe, Jim Scott, Tyler Todd, Dave Coen, Terry Cornelius, Mark Rabuse, Randy Latta, Bob McLeod, Dave Savage, Rich Kiblinger, David Conover and Kent Neubert.

The staff at Running Etc. in Norfolk, VA: Mike Robinson-owner, John Lamogda, Drew Midland, Doug Dugroo and Shannon Ralston.

Running partners: Bill Bernard, Greg Eck, Craig Allen, Dave McDonald, Ron Borsheim, Elwyn Davis, Dan Hurley, Ed Lee, David Kidd, Lee Lamonica, Sandy DiCarlo and Dudley Godoy.

Dr. David Young, Dr. James Dowd and Physician's Assistant, Ron Nave from the Jordan-Young Institute.

Anne Audain, Coach Roy Benson, Coach Roy Chernock, Lew Faxon, Pete Gibson, Brittany Gleeson, Josh Lee, Dr. Rudi Schuster, Charlie George and Jerry Bocrie.

Last but not least, Mel Williams, Ph.D. in Exercise Science. You were there for me during my good years and when I was unable to run, and encouraged me as I began running again.

Made in the USA
Charleston, SC
13 April 2014

about the *Author*

LAURA WARD is the author of UNTIL NOW, NOT YET, and PAST HEAVEN. She is also a co-author of THE PLEDGE, with Christine Manzari. Their second book in that series will be released this June, THE COLOR OF US. She lives in Maryland with her loud and very loving three children and husband. Laura married her college sweetheart and is endlessly grateful for the support he has given her through all their years together, and especially toward her goal of writing books. When not picking up toy trucks, driving to lacrosse practice, or checking spelling homework, Laura is writing or reading romance novels.

Contact Laura at:

www.facebook.com/LauraWardAuthor
Twitter — @laurarosnerward
Instagram — _Laura_Ward
Email — laurawardauthor@yahoo.com

65779028R00117

Made in the USA
Middletown, DE
03 March 2018